Ghosts of the Water

All rights reserved; no part of this book may be reproduced, stored in a retrieval system, or transmitted, in any form or by any means, without the prior permission in writing from the publisher, nor be otherwise circulated in any form of binding or cover other than that in which it is published and without a similar condition including this condition being imposed on the subsequent purchaser.

No generative artificial intelligence (AI) was used in the writing of this work. The author expressly prohibits any entity from using this publication for purposes of training AI technologies to generate text, including without limitation technologies that are capable of generating works in the same style or genre as this publication. The author reserves all rights to license use of this work for generative AI training and development of machine learning language models.

First published in Great Britain in 2025 by Turquoise Quill Press
an imprint of Not From This Planet

Copyright © 2025 by Elizabeth Lockwood
Cover Illustration by Lucja Fratczak-Kay
Interior Illustrations by Elizabeth Lockwood
Formatting by The Amethyst Angel

"Anemoia" and "Rebuilding"
First published in These Pages Sing, Autumn 2024, issue 01
thesepagessing.co.uk

"Due Date"
First published in These Pages Sing, Winter 2025, issue 02
thesepagessing.co.uk

ISBN: 978-1-912257-69-0

The moral right of the author has been asserted.

First Edition

Ghosts of the Water

poetry & illustrations
by
elizabeth lockwood

also by
elizabeth lockwood

non-fiction:

LITTLE SOMETHING

poetry:

Waves of Stardust

Rain and Leaves

for michelle,
my oldest and most
marvellously magical friend

ghosts of the water

The wind is whipping at the windows
A brown teddy bear from the RNLI gift shop
is lying on its side on the sofa
And the smell of the sea is lingering
Remnants of the sandy beach being deposited
on furniture and carpet
Rock pool nets, one green, one pink,
have been left by the back door
And shells have been placed in side pockets of a handbag,
which will be forgotten for over a week
A mug of hot coffee is being held in shaky hands
Starting to burn into palms
The noise of the waves crashing is ringing in ears
An aging spade snapped into two pieces in rain-soaked sand
and didn't make it home
And knots will need to be brushed out of windblown hair
Somehow these moments will be revisited in dreams
Like Instagram photos, snapshots in isolation
Gosh, it looked wonderful
Footprints in sand, running, dancing by the sea's edge
Dragging a shell through the sand to make letters
Smiles are wide but eyes are tired
Dwelling in an odd nostalgia,
little wishes flying through the air
Watching a plastic boat sail across a rock pool
But it never really saw the water

in quiet moments

Quiet moments breed
Memories which flash with a
Wicked vibrancy

Setting life on fire
With the voice of ignition
Behind our backs it

Burnt up hope slowly
Through our teeth clenched denial
Scorch marks still present

Vague ultrasound screen
Neither black or white just ash
The chip away of

Letters, emails, notes
Black print on white paper, lines
Fading with each read

The rosy-coloured
Words we had held onto smashed
To the ground, leaving

Sheer glass around us
Pieces scattered everywhere
Cutting ties with life

Time tied not only
Itself but us into the
Most intricate of

Knots, battered and frayed
At each aging strand, struggling
Against the riptide

Life and light drifted
Away like a little boat
On the vast blue sea

Leaving us stuck, pale-
Faced, meticulously lost
Sick from the stillness

Now present but not
Correct, colours no longer
Complement each mood

They bleed into the
Ocean, where the boat cannot
Be seen by earth's eyes

The quiet moments
Keep letting it all back in
Playing it all out

Again, piece by piece
But it never ever makes
A brand new ending

circuit breaker

Can I turn the clock back a couple of hours
And then pause the scene in front of me
Instead of deciding to make a point
Just letting it go
Letting it flow
Because you didn't mean any harm
Just fixated by a task
And I wanted to move it on
Wanted to show you, you were wrong
And now I am sad and tired
Of always making mistakes
Watching the cycle spin round and round
Always trying but tripping over laces
I have forgotten to tidy away

Snapping off fibre optic connections
Plucking from soil roots
But not on purpose
Because the clock ties us up in knots
It drains and it scratches away
Trying to nurture and build
Synapses, cells, overflow
Then pulling the rug by
Trying to be an echo of the past
Which I can't seem to shrug off
This is where the battle lies
Between deeply ingrained experience
Expectations, what I think I'm meant to be
Clashing with what we know now,
what we feel now
Who we are now

Changing experience, example,
all the things that I've known
So mistakes aren't tumbling around the same cycle
To make new, to make free
What I would really like is to throw it all
Into the recycling bin, blue and green
To drown it all in healing waters
Before picking out who I am, who I want to be
And pegging it on the line, on your synapses
It's easy to lose sight of you when panic kicks in
When the clock grasps both wrists
Forcing a dam in the flow of thought evolution
Breathing deep and allowing muddy boots to squelch
and unpick themselves from glue floor
To help foster your mind, your being
While letting the stone weight of old programming go

the faces we paint

I think about being a child
And the superlative joy of having
Your face covered with paint
To be a tiger, or a flower or a superhero

I think about being an adult
And the exhaustion of painting
On happiness, or togetherness or I'm okay
Yet feeling none of these things inside

I think about being a child
And slowly learning to hide
Emotions are too big, feelings too strong
Building up a mask, face paint slowly turning into armour

I think about being an adult
And trying to undo what's already
Been learnt, fed up of that aching smile
But worrying what everyone else will think

your name

Leaves say your name
When falling and rustling
Echoing your life on every fading line

Rain taps your name
On glass and ground
Dropping your memory into fertile soil

Birds sing your name
In poetry and prose
Wings carving your story through the sky

Waves write your name
With sand and pebbles
Spreading your love through every ocean

arrivals / departures

There were ants in the sugar
Big, fat ants crawling through the crystalline substance
Plastic spoon gravestones
and phantom steam billowing
And there were trains arriving and leaving
and just sitting there
With feet tapping and huffs being exhaled
by people wanting to be anywhere else but there

There were flies in the ointment
Small, black and beating their wings for release
Dots joining together to write a tragedy
And there were people arriving and leaving
and just sitting there
With breath catching and nails digging
by patients wanting to be anywhere else but there

There were moths in the wardrobe
Big, grey and dormant, biding their time to take flight
Banging against their chosen tomb, splintering fragile bodies
And there were thoughts arriving and leaving
and just sitting there
With images flashing and words nagging
by souls wanting to be anywhere else but there

redo

Can we redo Christmas?
Because I don't think there was enough magic in it
I don't think anyone enjoyed themselves
as much as they could have
I don't think it lived up to the ideas in my head very well
I don't think anyone will look back with bubbling nostalgia
and wish to live in the memory forever

Can we redo your birthday?
Because I'm not sure you really enjoyed it enough
I'm not sure your smiles were quite wide enough
I don't think it lived up to those old photographs I've seen
Of hysterical laughter and eyes alive with a dream

Can we redo last weekend?
Because honestly it was a bit of a bore
No one seemed to have much fun
I don't think anyone was as creative or productive
or as loving as they should have been
It didn't quite live up to the polished
and perfect posts I've seen online
Where rain suits and wellies and mud
and perfect cakes and crafts and hashtags reside

chaos

The seasons are changing
What once was green is becoming yellow
Getting ready to brown and fall
Nights are darkening, drawing themselves closer
Children are ready to start a new year
Their bags stocked
Their lunchboxes full
And the order of the world is being followed
As it always is
But to me it just feels
Like chaos

halloween in the in-between

On the day and night in which the veil becomes thinner
When you can almost breathe in the place that exists
Just out of our reach
We've come to the place where we took him
Where the trees outnumber the words of visitors
And where anxiety bubbles like a simmering cauldron
Because we remember being here before
Expecting his life to spread its wings before us
But then it didn't
And now we've brought another one here too
Just like him
But without phone calls of news and test results
A witch's broom hovers mid-air
Waiting for the confidence to fly
And I wonder do you know each other
Do your souls meet in the place we cannot see?
When we carve the pumpkins today
With rosy cheeks and spider webs
Hands cold from throwing fallen leaves
On Halloween in the in between
Then and now will merge and we will all be together
One will kick and shift position, almost ready
One will flicker like candle light, lingering ghost-like but warm
And the others will giggle with a delight
that holds a knowing beyond their young years

home

I can feel you moving
Shifting position
A delicate bone click
As you get comfy
Because I'm your home
You only know me
And I hope that any bad day outside
Won't cross over
Only safety, only love
Should reach you
In your home

birth/death certificate

No one ever imagines holding
A death certificate for their child
Birth certificates remain tucked away
In a box or a file of important papers
Maybe misplaced and searched for frantically
On occasion
But no parent should ever hold their child's death certificate
With black type in its finality
Cause of death
Time of death
A death no parent should ever see or experience
Contained within two sides of an A4 sheet of paper
We might imagine holding a marriage certificate one day
Or an educational certificate
And be full to the brim with joy for a little life grown big
But not death
Not birth and death together
Just left with certificates to file away safe
So that when another morning dawns
And the traces of you are only heard in echoes
And the world has decided to keep ticking
These papers not only prove you died
But also lived

where?

Where did your first taste of milk fade away to?
Where did your first breath of fresh air disappear to?
Where did your first smile slip away to?
Where did your first steps across the living room floor
drift off to?
Where did your first word fade away to?
Where did your first dance disappear to?
Where did your first day of school slip away to?
Where did your first job drift off to?
Where did your first love fade away to?
Where did your first child go?
Where did your life go?

on the edge

Leaves may rain in the last days of autumn
Just as the air turns wintry and ready for frost
When fairy lights are switched on to cheer the dark skies
And lists are written and posted and gifts are bought
and wrapped and hidden
Ready for the approaching joy
and candle-warm glow of December
And I want to breathe in the magic of the season,
which will soon flood the earth
But I can't stop seeing the sadness everywhere
Tingeing even the rosiest moment
Because I want more than his spirit nestled alongside us
And I can't stop seeing the emptiness,
the places where he should be
But I'll stumble on and I'll go through the motions
Minute by minute, day by day
Until I realise, until I see
That even though he is not here with me
Every stocking, every space, every moment
Will always be full with our love

idyllic

I hope you know just how much I love you
If I could, I would change the world for you
Piece by piece until you felt whole, felt safe
If I could, I would rewrite the skies for you
For rain to call off play or for blue to drown out grey
If I could, I would turn back the clocks for you
Make different decisions, carve out a different mould
Keep your beautiful smiling face going,
ensuring no sadness could ever take hold
If I could, I would rub out the lines for you
Help you see past mistakes
Help patch up the cracks in your heart if it breaks

If I could, I would
I would
If I could

empty cot

Sleeping next to an empty cot holds more than one meaning
It's a gap being bridged between the one that should be here and the one that soon will be
The in between
Where life and death are connected
Where fear and love hold hands
And where hope and grief sleep in the same bed

driving home

So small, yet quite a weight
You came snuffling into our lives
Taken away for a while, to be encased in clear plastic
To have tubes all over you
As I regained the feeling in my legs
and took to my feet to get to you
I watched you take it all in your stride
My c-section wound seeming inconsequential
And back you came
With only the sound of clear breathing remaining
With cuddles and milk sick and blue lined nappies
And we went home
After medication, after monitoring was done
Cannulas removed
Daddy driving us in the dark
Ready to meet your big brother and sisters
For them to cover you with their excitement and love
And I sobbed guttural tears
In the dark, with the street lamps flashing by
Highlighting your sleeping face
Because you were coming home
But he, your other big brother
Never got to

empty arms become full

When empty arms become full
They still ache
With the shadows of grief, with the echoes of pain
And they simultaneously hold death and life
With the new warmth of a beating heart nestled in
And the gentle inhale and exhale of healthy lungs
With the old memory of quiet and stillness
And watching life drain away with laboured breaths, replaying and replaying
Those arms that have held life and death
Will never stop aching

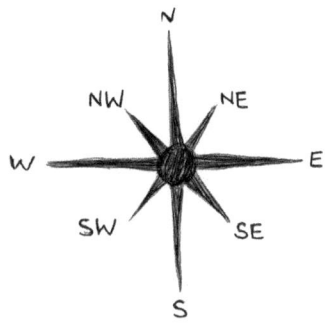

happy new year

Happy New Year! they shout
As the old turns to new
And clean pages of diaries are opened
Ready for another year
But I don't want a fresh start
I want to go back in time
And embed myself into an old calendar
With edges curling with age and ink fading
To be with you again

the trouble with birthdays

The trouble with birthdays is

That while we get to moan about
more grey hair
too many candles to fit on a cake
newly found wrinkles
what we've done or not done with another passing year
what we'd like to unwrap
or who we'd like to see
or where we'd like to go to

You don't get to grow out of
your baby clothes
or crib or pram
or cast old toys aside ready for new
or eat your first piece of birthday cake
or have a party where you're here, giddy and excited,
ripping wrapping paper with bemusement

You don't get to live
And we get to take life for granted

over and over again

Grief creeps up in bright sunlight
Whispers its lead balloon words
Flashes its images, kaleidoscopic and stomach turning
And I am breathless and devastated
All over again

privilege

Summer is packing its bags to go on its well-earned break
It's going to put its feet up and rest
And we are going to pack different bags
Filled with lunchboxes and pencil cases
As autumn has just been biding its time
And we are going to start the car to drive to a building through the same frustrating traffic
Because we cannot be late
They won't get their attendance award
And we can't forget
Because they need to take in a pound for something today
Or they need their wellies
Or it's PE or something. It's always something
And we will all hang on until October half term
When we can bask in the falling leaves
And pumpkins and invite ghosts to tea

Then watch as the days countdown to Christmas
As winter will be waiting in the wings
When it'll become obvious how much more they know
Every day out or book read together will show on their faces
And their nativity play will make each traffic jam worth it
And we will feel a funny sadness inside
Acknowledging the passage of time
And the new year will roll in ready to repeat the cycle
But what a privilege it is
To watch them grow

ghosts

Courage would not exist without fear
All fuelled by love that will never disappear
The light that trailed in your wake
Has been set ablaze by new life yet dampened
by a familiar ache

Overwhelming and wonderful and frightening
Tiptoeing and turbulent and sudden like lightning
Lost in the ballerina twirl, sick from the motion
Gulping air but just breathing in the ocean

Fleetingly longing for the safety of life before
But draped in a love that's ludicrous to ignore
The words are whispered on the evening air
And I'm hanging on tightly to prayer

Worrying that the bird singing in the night will stop its song
The stars start looking like chaos, all mixed up and wrong
I'm afraid every time I look at your face
That heartbreak will again tear through this place

Heart racing with jumbled thoughts as the day turns to night
Willing the threatening darkness to burst
with the brightest light
And pushing forward anyway
But inviting ghosts to stay

730 days

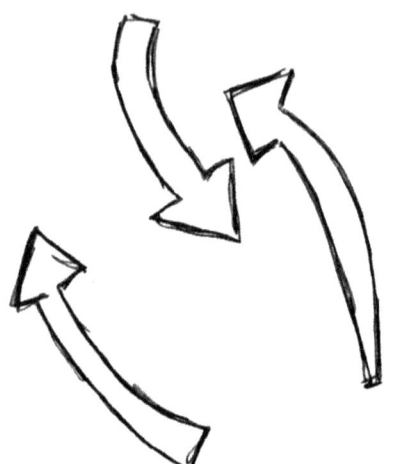

In the lead up to yet another significant date
I find myself languishing, alternating between numbness
and deep, deep pain
Where that stomach punch of grief
takes a couple of breaths
and pricks tears around each eye,
and either I let go and sob
Or the refusal to feel anything takes over
To get on, to get things done,
to not have to feel so much all the time
I know why people try to ignore grief
Because it hurts so very much
No matter how much time elapses
I look at your photos
Hanging on the wall or gracing the tops of shelves
And each day you've been gone
Weighs down on each shoulder
until I'm waist deep in concrete grief
730 days soon approaches
But it feels like only yesterday we were together

vodka

Your home was built
By the bones of others
With paper and coin
Falling like unexpected rain

Your health was ruined
By the decision to live
For today alone
Drinking like you've never seen water

Your faith was shattered
By the loss of the heart of the home
With warm embrace missing
Breaking like brittle branches

spilled words

The winter soil aches
Spilled words join the bulbs and seeds
Green shoots ruminate
They protrude from the cold earth
Some things won't remain buried

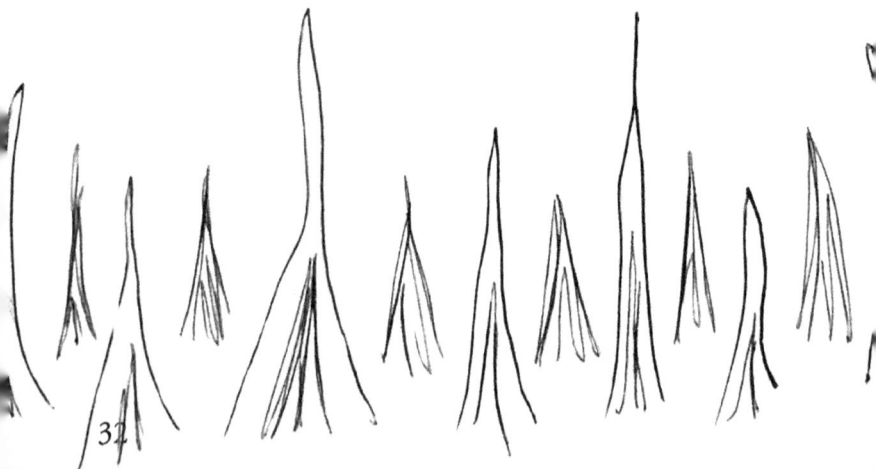

two

Those soft pink lines
Wove themselves into the evening sky
Everything aglow as the night waited
Its turn
And I stood next to dirty dishes and a newly baked cake
Brimming with too many thoughts and emotions
Searching the skies
As if it was Christmas Eve
For a trace of you

ash

The smoke from your ashes filled the whole town
But only I could see it

Everyone was breathing it in
But only I could feel it

The echo from your last words filled every frequency
But only I could hear it

Everyone was imbibing it
But only I could perceive it

The chasm from your exit filled every moment
But only I could know it

Everyone was tripping over it
But only I could live in it

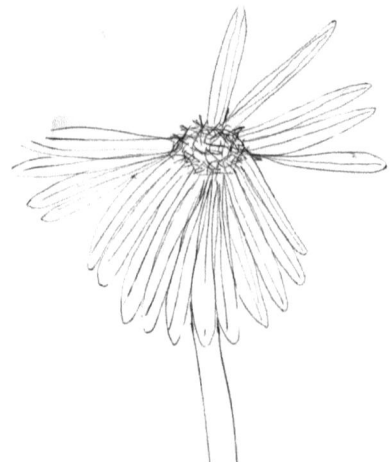

both sides

Living in the frustration of
Everything
And nothing
Sleeping alongside the anger of
Everyone
And no one
Getting lost in the fog of grief
Everywhere
And nowhere

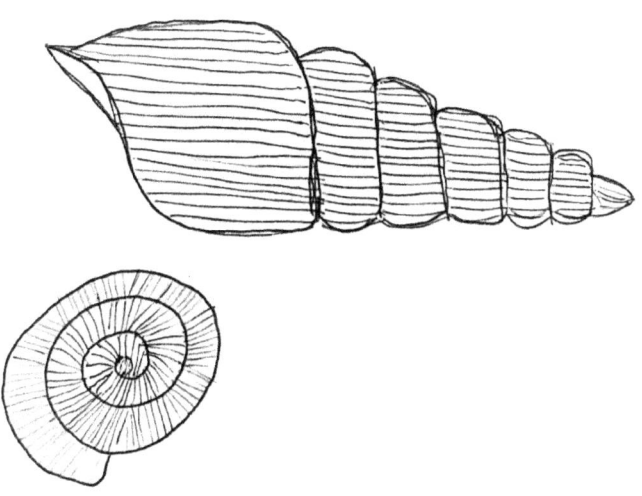

fleeting

Is that you triggering the security light again?
Pressing your face up against the glass of the door
Acting like it was just the wind
But I heard you calling my name
As I stirred a pot full of carrots bubbling
Am I really pretending that sudden icy air
came from the window vents?
I can see you moving the leaves of the trees
and causing the branches to sway
I can feel you slip past as you walk in the door
Yet I keep brushing this all away
Because in a flash you're gone again
I never get the chance to invite you to stay

Maybe my tears
Will water the seeds of your memory
And you'll be too full of blossom
To be forgotten

stay

Breathing in the top of your head

As you lie against my chest

Full from milk

And tired from kicking your legs and reaching for hanging toys

Holding you that little bit closer

As a passing thought shakes my core

I don't want to be afraid

I just want you to stay

With me

You illuminate my path
Like the stars in the sky
The darkness cannot win
As your light will never dim

thinking of you

I found a little feather on the bookshelf
White flecked with greyish brown
In front of books that I probably enjoy
more than the children do
Of orange tigers and big grey tabby cats
How it got there I don't know
Did I find it somewhere else
and then put it in the catch-all pot
on top of the bookcase
or the kitchen windowsill
Which I am prone to do
Only for the wind to sneak its way under the softness
and carry it through the air
To settle below

Or did a child on tiptoe reach and move it
Or was it new
Carried in by the spirit of you
Trying to tell me
You are right
I am here
And I love you so
And does it matter either way?
It still made me gaze at your photos
Heartstrings tugged like shoe laces
Emotion caught, freed or not freed
It still made me think of you

reluctance

Busy while viewing the cities floating in the breeze
Hitching a ride on a feather to answer the call home

So please come home

Rummaging around my insides for a 16-piece dinner set
Your intrusiveness pours the teapot

And my reluctance scurries like a rat up a drainpipe

Kicking cans up the river or road or racetrack
Holding onto the barrier at the ice rink

But you already let go

glimpse of heaven

That time with you
That teeny tiny piece of time
Was a glimpse of heaven
Overwhelming pure love
That reverberates though

    every second

                    minute

       hour

                       day

     week

          month

                 year

     since

trouble

Do you know what your trouble is?
You let every thought show itself on your face
You furrow your brows
And narrow your eyes
You stare in horror like you've seen something
you can't unsee
You bite down on your bottom lip in anguish, in anxiety
You raise your eyebrows and push your cheeks out
at the absurd
And even at rest the lines on your face
Tell the story of your inner world
Scribbles that you can't erase
You need to stop pulling faces
That's your trouble

wtf

Wilful words wallow in sanity
While I wait wrestling and writhing
Watching the wishing well water ripple and
Waiting for the warmth of wonder to
Weave its weatherproof wrap around my mind despite
Whispering nothing but wicked warning

These thoughts are terrible and turbulent
Teaming with tiny thunderstorms
Ticking with too many tempers and
Trying to tighten knots and taint
The tincture, the balm, the treat
Those troublesome letters, tangible and tireless

Futures fall down in fear
Fraying fabric edges in furore
Fighting as failure looms, inviting
Forest branches and flowers to flow and
Foster fair-minded feelings yet never forgetting the
Fatigue and fascination, but forging to be finally free

i still look for you

I still look for you
In my rear view mirror when I'm driving
Even though you never sat in a car seat
I half expect to see you there
Fascinated by the scenes rushing past the window
Or rain drops slithering
Or mist from our breath, slowly creeping over the glass
That glance back is a jolt
To the present, to the sinking stomach
To that feeling of words being stolen by an interruption, mouth half open, frozen
To that thing I already knew
That you died not long after you were born
These moments are fundamental, they're soul level, they come from the core
With that uncontrollable ache
And I know you're not there but
I still look for you

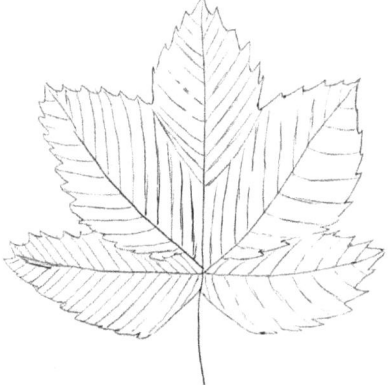

give

Give us strength
Give us love
Give us light
Give us the will to carry on
Help us shelter from not only the storm
But the quiet
The calm

if hope fails
then we will still have won

There's a flicker
A tiny seed, filled with light
Even though the drought is rife
Water still flows
And the seed is turning green with
Little shoots, desperate to grow
Sending love, spreading joy through roots
If we pray, if we beg, if we screw our eyes tight and shout
Maybe this hope will emerge through the soil
And let healing light overflow

But
if hope fails
And nothing shows
We will still have won
Because of the goodness it gave
To the earth

so many

So many stars, so many days
So many mother's tears
Spilled over keyboards
Spilled over steering wheels
So many lives, so many prayers
So many mother's fears
Played out over hospital stays
Played out over unanswered calls
So many prayers, so many lives
So many days, so many stars

resurrection

The skies become bluer
And the green more vibrant
Nature is coming back to life
With a spring in its awakening step
And the world is full with the resurrection
Empty tomb and hollow chocolate eggs
Stone rolled and light abundant
But your body continues to lie in the ground
And doesn't bloom with the flowers
Or rise with the sun
Only your spirit lives with us
Which I grasp and cling to
Like the roots in the soil
Entangled and connected in darkness and light

love

Mugs of strong coffee
Tired yawns and warm cuddles
If they could bottle this exhaustion
They'd also encapsulate love

searching

I expected to find you in the symbolic
In the embryonic and in the hyperbolic
In the feather, the robin in the trees,
in the lines of the leaves, I was right

But I also find you just out of sight
In the night and in the light
In a feeling, in a curious moment,
in a delicate whisper, an unearthly tonic,
sometimes melancholic, maybe even shambolic

This grief has taken flight
And this love is alight

muse

I don't want to write about the outrage
And the peeling back of layers
Protecting cores or screaming words
As they've already been written about
Each tear inducing layer, each red-eyed rant
By someone else, somewhere else
But I want to write about pale blue petals
On flowers planted in hope in black soil
The period of silence before breath is taken
and crying becomes a celebration
About the foam that tops a rousing espresso
And the moment the sun drenches through the darkness
As morning decides it's time to rise
And the dragging back of a wave over sand and stone,
the glass that smashes, the fragility, the tide
And that tear producing flood
Of longing that picks away
At threads, at the seams
At the fabric of each step forward
Of each moment of duality and each heartbeat since
Even though they've already been written about
Somewhere else, by someone else

never changing

I haven't sat here with a coffee for some time
The angle is slightly different
As is the seating
But the way the sea lies there seems never changing
The ghosts remain below the waves
The trees have a gentle sway
Holding themselves up to the sky
Acting like a mirror for your soul
Warm coffee tastes that little bit more bitter
The tiptoes across the decking are just out of reach
And the wildflowers remain out of control

what's to come

Scrolling through old photos
Of little grins and fairy lights
And wide smile delights
A breath suddenly stops, and I stare
A photo of my eldest son,
Cheeky eyed and magic strewn
He stands by the Christmas tree
Full of wonder, plain to see
With a brown reindeer clasped
Between his little hands
And I breathed out a knowing discomfort
Because a few years later he would grasp
A different reindeer in his hands
On a Christmas where the magic had subdued
All day and all night
Sparkling and white
Representing our little deer
His baby brother who left the world
Too soon
And he held that reindeer like it connected
Their souls
And I looked back at the twinkles in his toddler eyes
The foreshadows colourful and bright
Fate focused on a different view
And I thought of what was to come and said
thank God we never knew

reminders
Please don't hide the light
Send us reminders of your
Luminosity

light
Wonderful and bright
So beautifully you rise
Overwhelming light

forget-me-not
I see you growing
Through barren tarmac, spreading
beauty regardless

peace
It is exhausting
Waiting for more disaster
May we have peace now

rain

The morning rain drips,
drops, splashes, on growing leaves
It wakes up my soul

broken home

They say home is what
You make it, so why must mine
Be so incomplete

magic

The way the colours
Decorate the sky always
Feels like your magic

spread your wings

It is time to grow
Nature calls you to immerse
Yourself in the light

Sunflowers

They are luminous
Their light and love
 radiates
Everywhere we look

equal

I will love him in
Heaven as I love them on
Earth, for love is equal

treasure

I held a seashell
Up to my ear, but I heard
More than just the sea

lost again

Whenever I think
I've found a little peace, it
Slips through my fingers

hiding

The light nights make life
Brighter but they make me want
To draw the curtains

creative battle

Art is still art if
One person sees its beauty
Or one million do

light & dark

The light punctuates
The dark sky with wonder, I
See you in each spark

blossom trees

You didn't stay for long
But while you were here you were
So magnificent

spring clean

Time for some cleansing breaths
I want to spring clean all these
Intrusive thoughts again

your light

I keep fairy lights
Up all year round. Their sparkle
Reminds me of you

puddles

Splash with the raindrops
Send waves of your laughter to
Fill the world with joy

snap

Old photographs make
Me nostalgic, even when
They've captured sadness

softly spoken

The wind whispers to
the trees telling them secrets
We're not meant to hear

bee sting

The sudden sting snaps
Like a twig or my temper
But won't fly away

clean slate

I tried to wipe the
Slate clean, but I could still see
The same reflections

you can never tell

Try not to snap with
Your judgements, you never know
What lies underneath

new growth

You may blossom here
Under the spring morning sun
You are safe to grow

early bird

I'm up with the sun
To see if I can capture
The early bird's song

tulips

Beautifully concise
Those orange tulips grow tall
Vibrant, just like you

survival

Fallen petals wilt
In our fight for survival
Peace begs us to stop

never ending

On Earth or Heaven
This love is never ending
We are forever

hope

I will write letters
In ink, in sand and in frost
The words give me hope

silver & gold

The silver moon gives way
For the golden sun to shine
Morning wakes the earth

sudden storm

The news crashed around
More sudden than any storm
Thunder still echoes

confession

The ground swallowed me
And all the words I needed
For my confession

sing

Right or wrong, it's time
To sing your sweet song out loud
Let's hope for the best

indigo

Neither here nor there
Living in the in between
Neither dark nor light

exit sign

No easy way out
Exists on this path forward
We must keep going

sea spray

The spray falls like rain
While storms loom over the sea
Waves overwhelm me

holding on

I hold this feeling
In both of my shaking hands
I will not let go

ocean memories

The sea doesn't tell lies
But the waves do tell stories
I treasure yours most

sorry about the broken lawn mower

Our feet crunched the gravel path
With each step
The noise overwhelming the silence
The sun glinted through tree branches
As it started to set
And the happiness of a holiday
Was marred with a quiet sadness
Our ears were full of
The audible absence of pram wheels being pushed
Over chipped grey stone
But we walked along anyway
Getting used to this feeling, used to this reality
We would later form his name from gravel pieces
And leave them on the grass bank
On another path nearby
So that the world would see his name
And know that he was with us too

nocturnal nostalgia

Nocturnal nostalgia pulls at my insides
Through bright sunlight or grey cloud
To where the night has fallen
Where sometimes I close the curtains to keep it out
And bathe in artificial light
And other times I let the dark swirl through each room
And stare

That desire for the quiet
For the darkness, for the stars
For the chance to sit in silence
Away from the constant, the busyness, the out of control
And watch thoughts drift across my sight
Or to mindlessly watch images on the television screen go by
To mull over things from the past, relive and rethink

That want to tiptoe through the hush
To open doors tentatively
To slink like a cat in the dark
Jumping to a high perch to watch each star in the sky
Until a passing cloud tells me that's enough now
But just hanging on, to have that little bit more
Before sleep comes to reset it all

same name

Walking with the spring blossom
And the greening trees
With the huff and puff of an afternoon walk
Smiling with each robin that flies by or lands in view
Then pausing breath and motion upon hearing
Your name being called by someone else, to someone else
With sadness creeping up as we watched another boy,
full of life
Running with ash brown hair billowing back
Rosy cheeks and glinting eyes
And the thought hits and keep hitting
Same name but full of death
Ash brown hair without movement
But he would've? Should've?
This is what we're missing
This is what he's missing
Running with a carelessness
Through the greening trees
And spring blossom
Huffing and puffing with a flushing face
And eyes full of sparks

maybe

Maybe that was the
wrong choice. Maybe those were the
right decisions. Maybe.

Maybe I'll ruin
the present, trying to revise
the past. Maybe.

that girl

I remember being that girl
Legs crossed with pins and needles
Footstool rest for my dinner plate
And the same video on repeat
The VCR whir my company

I remember being that girl
Imaging futures brighter
Than the midday sun
Wondering when things would take off
Eyes focused on the sky

I remember being that girl
Embarrassed about my size
Fed of always being the fat kid
Wanting to fall asleep and wake up thin
But unable to stop eating

I remember being that girl
Scared of rejection
Outwardly boisterous
Inwardly terrified
Living and breathing anxiety

I remember being that girl
Watching dreams and desires
Fall like rain but then drip down drains
Lost amongst forgotten ideas
Believing things just weren't possible

I remember being that girl
The one that just wanted to be loved
To feel normal, accepted
Scribbling words on paper
Then ripping them all to pieces

I remember being that girl
Perched on the breakfast bar stool
Birthday goldfish lying dead
Worried the house was going to burn down
Torn between two families

wishes

I made a wish with
A black pen on white paper
I shared it with the night sky
Asked the stars to help
I hope it came true
And our love was sent to you

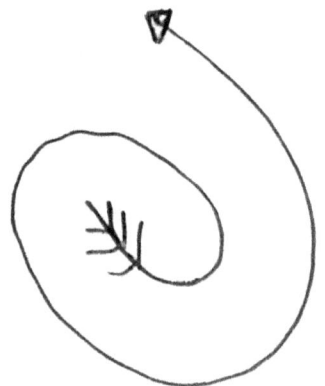

sleeping awake

Sometimes I look back
On that time, like it was just
A vivid dream, where

Nothing made sense and
It all kept getting worse, yet
I did not wake up

So either I am
Still asleep, or this nightmare
Happened in real life

And maybe I will
Never find out, no matter
How much time flies by

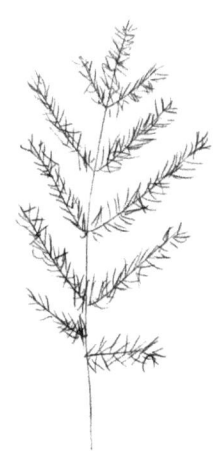

due date

Pretending that we walked along wooded paths, pausing to hear messages carried on the wings of blackbirds and robins

Brushing my fingertips along all the evergreen growth, feeling the smooth and the rough, breathing deeply and talking to you in rhyme

Draining from explaining, exhausted from holding on to future thoughts, unable to face the overwhelming light of outdoors any longer

Sitting glued to the sofa, praying desperately, mindlessly staring, or driving, listening to the radio but only hearing the same song

Focusing on the flames in the fireplace, sure that an image would appear, watching the wind take the ash away, hoping it would also take the fear

Watching the sun setting over the sea and town, the colour disappearing to blackness, spending time holding your imaginary hand

Writing your name on each star as they emerged through the kitchen window, marking a cross on my forehead with coal dust

Drowning my hands in the washing up bowl, while the water spilled over the sides, flooding the whole house

mementoes

All we have left of you
Is placed inside a memory box
How can a life so vast
How can a soul so big
Be reduced into so little

all for you

We find pretty stones, shells and feathers
We bring them home
Or take them to your grave
As if they are presents
For you

We take photographs of your name
Written in sand or stone or ink
Or your teddy, in places we go
To make new memories
For you

We tell your story, create art
Walk along with you everyday
Or run, hand in hand
Doing all we can to live
For you

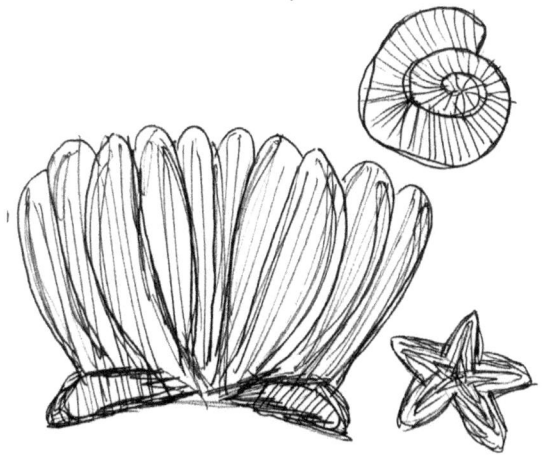

Opening the kitchen door
to replace the air
To swap the energies
And the fairies fly in
To invade our home
with their
spring magic

sleepless

I'll kiss the top of your head
As you nap in my arms, tired from night-time waking
I'll drink strong coffee
From the biggest mug I can find and
I'll yawn my way through the morning
Smiling as you hold onto my hand
I'll say gosh I hope you sleep better tonight
But you'll still be my favourite reason to be sleepless

facebook notifications

Facebook told me it was your birthday
But you haven't been alive to see it
For six years
I wonder how many notifications keep
Mounting themselves up
On your dormant account
Still active but not active at all
I wonder if there are people on your friends list
That don't know you died
Just think you don't post anymore
Just quietly observing
And those that do
I wonder if they can see you
In the lilac sky or the clouds
That keep passing by

blooming

The new blooms bask in
the morning sunlight, stretching
With life below ground forgotten
they inhale the warmth

Before the afternoon rain comes
to drench their roots
Soil blackening like the night sky,
stems holding up the weight of each drop

Later, the dark night covers them, safe and quiet,
they sleep until dawn
When the gentle breeze will wake them
and dry their swaying petals

a joyful return

The spring flowers are
Making a joyful return
Sharing their goodness

Not just with the world
But with our exhausted souls
As a beautiful gift

holiday snaps

I think we all used to be better at waiting
We could finish a roll of film,
rewind and take it to be developed
Then wait
Gratification or disappointment wasn't instant
And it wasn't digital
It was tangible and arrived in a paper envelope
Ready to be looked through with laughs or groans
Red eyed or blurred or underexposed
Or the perfect moment captured
through meticulous posing or accidental snap
Grouping around and saying,
Oh remember when that happened
And the absolute favourites might make it
Into frames,
while the rest were lovingly placed in an album or box
To wait for us to look through them again

future plans

How can I make plans
for future endeavours when
I want the ghost of

the past to keep me
company in the present
To hold my hand and

retell our stories
Repeating the words over
And over again

wading

I don't know why some days
Grief is really heavy
Like I'm knee deep in mud
Trying to wade through

And other days it's lighter
Thoughts are a little bit quieter
And I can walk with ease
But it's never as light as a feather

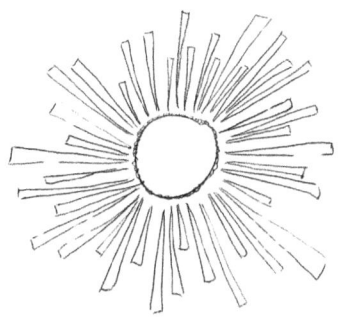

emergency

When the stars emerged
I searched, not just the darkening sky,
But my heart
For a reminder of your light

When the sun started to rise
I wished, not just for your presence,
But for life
For everything to be alright

When the moon was hidden by clouds
I asked, not just for a miracle,
But for love
For your beauty to be in sight

face paint

The humid air of the Spanish summer
Fills the entertainment space
Of the hotel of a first holiday abroad
Four years old, long brown hair,
fringe sticking to a slightly clammy forehead
Loud music and kids bouncing off the walls
The girls all wearing grass skirts
Colours of reds and browns
They must have given them out
Swishing around knees with each step or sway
And queuing and waiting and queuing and waiting
For a lady to apply face paint to eager little faces
She had long blonde hair and chunky bangles and earrings
I'm watching little girl after little girl sit
and have their faces painted by
The lady, the very lovely-looking lady,
and she's telling each girl how cute she is or how beautiful,
sometimes kissing their cheeks
before sending them on their way
Making a fuss that would bring a smile
to even the moodiest of faces
Thoughts spinning round an immature mind
I wonder what she'll say to me, I want that fuss,
I want to be pretty

The music keeps playing, the songs make the adults groan,
the children think it's wonderful
Small feet tiptoe up, as my turn has arrived
And I sit ready to feel like the others did, ready to glow
And she works, silently, applies the paint and says,
okay there you go
But instead of getting up, there's a pause, a wait,
hanging on to be told, oh you're adorable
But only an awkward look is given
No words join the music
I just stare at her, willing her to say something nice
But all there is
Is just the sinking of a little heart,
learning then and there that she's not beautiful,
she's not cute, and she's not adorable
But the other girls are
And off the small feet go, to join her mum, her sister
To stand for her mother to photograph her with her sister
Humid faces, grass skirts and no smile
Feeling like crying, but saying nothing
Because why should this lady matter to a four year old,
why does not being included in praise matter,
why does not being told they're beautiful matter,
beauty is on the inside, isn't it?
Looks don't matter, do they?

Why do you need to be told you're cute? A delight?
Why did I even want the fuss?
Why does it even matter?
If it doesn't really matter then why
Have I not forgotten it?
Why do I still remember how it made me feel?
Just a small moment in time and space
Just some makeup all over my face

being good

Your goodness graces Earth
At just the right moment
Raining down invisible sparks
Sending love from Heaven
To refuel our stores of hope

missing

Even the best family photograph
When everyone's looking the same way
With smiles, a funny face or laugh
On the beach, in the woods or just a sunny day
Will be tinged with that special kind of sadness
As he's obviously missing in every way

the moon tonight

Early morning moon shines in sight
Above the din of awakening birds
As if it wants to know why
It wasn't noticed during the quiet of night
When it reflected across the water
Trying to tell us stories
Almost full to the brim with its magic light

summer holidays

Our precious moments are many
Full of seaside ice cream and long woodland walks
Sunny skies and boisterous laughter
Rain showers and running for cover
Playing games and making up silly jokes
Watching films and repeating TV shows
With big squishy cuddles
But sometimes we're tired and grumpy
Or fierce like a tiger, arguing over this and that
He or she isn't willing to tidy up
But little storms pass quickly
Because we love fiercely too
And everyone's happy to be together
Even when there's nothing to do

time off

I don't want time off
From grief or love
I just want
To walk forward and
Take you with me

baby steps

The path twists and turns
Yet even with these small steps
Time keeps passing by
We keep going forward but
We never leave you behind

summer's breath

Though the sky is grey
I can feel the air changing
Flowers are blooming
Summer's breath is flowing through
Stirring every earthly soul

forgotten smiles

Old photographs of
life before trauma, hold all
my forgotten smiles

I don't remember
happiness without sadness
Tingeing every smile

31st may

The last day of May
Was final for more than one reason
The hope that was once in excess
Waned to a slow drip
The last of the forget-me-nots had bloomed
And a life's worth of framed photographs
Started to look a little sad
Everyone knew that time would stop
At any moment
And this world would melt away
Overpowered by light
But only for him

grandfather & grandson

Two candles were lit
One for a grandfather who didn't get to meet
His grandchildren on Earth
And one for a grandson
Who didn't get to live on Earth for long
They exist where light is abundant
Where love is infinite
And the sadness of grief is just a whisper
Surrounded by joy and wonder
Spending the time together in Heaven
That was missed on Earth

parenting

How can I parent someone
Who is no longer here
Who doesn't live on Earth

How do I keep their memory alive
When their name, their life
Fades out of the thoughts of other people

How will I ensure that they are always included
Always counted in our family
Always visible in the invisible

I don't know
But I'm trying to

running

Will you run with me?
It might be the hardest race
Of your life so far
But we will feel the fresh air
On our tired faces
And breathe in life
Precious life

petals

I wrote a message on a rose petal
Dropped it in the flowing water
Watched it dance along each crest
Snaking around the twisting stream
Until it was gone from my sight
And I prayed that when it arrived
At your feet from the crystal clear sea
You would not only read the message
But feel all the love that came from me

cloudy skies

I've got a soft spot
For cloudy skies holding imminent rain
For someone to tut and say, I hope the weather behaves
And reflective grey seas
Ready to crash their waves
So that someone walking along the seafront will comment
It's looking choppy today
I excel at knowing how to live in the brooding storm
Where you don't have to pretend it's all okay
I feel a warmth from the blustery wind
or the tipping down rain
It's almost a relief when it's a horrible day
The sort that makes people say,
have you seen the weather out there
Yes the rain is falling in drops that contain the future
Looks like we'll have to cancel our plans,
yet secretly I don't care

best friend

From the top of the sky
To the bottom of the sea
Grey or blue, doesn't matter to me
I am happy to just be with you
However that may be
Laughing or crying or venting
It's all welcome with me

ask and you shall not receive

I talk to the moon
In the midnight sky
I ask it to tell me its secrets
How I can walk this winding path
With only a candlelight glow for guidance
I ask and I ask again
I can only pretend to understand
Why silence is the only answer
And why life remains unplanned

ripped paper

I wrote some words on paper
In black ink, poignant and deliberate
I ripped them to shreds, small like confetti
Before throwing them in the air
Closing my eyes to not see where they fell
Hoping the words would find a new home
And leave me alone

green

I keep planting seeds
To replace all the darkness
With green growth and light

Yet the dark creeps in
No matter what I scatter
Hope is out of sight

But I will dig down
And the seeds will grow so wild
With a glow so bright

One day the garden
Will overflow with tall trees
I will win this fight

takeaway coffee

A blank stare and a takeaway coffee
Numbness swallowed with each sip
I don't know why I missed this so much
Because now I can have it
It's only bitterness and froth
It's only swirled with saccharine sweet
And I could take it or leave it

repetition

Tell me a story
I'll repeat it back to you
Round and round we go

Tell you a story
You repeat it back to me
Round and round we go

Tell them a story
They repeat it back to us
Round and round we go

sweet treats

Rain hits the sand and we run for cover
But the ice cream van still beckons
With its siren call from rusting edges
The car is drier but not at all warmer
The rain has dripped big ice cream drops
On us, on the seats, acting like glue
Staining more than we can see
Now the wind is whipping up the day
and tapping it against the windscreen
Throwing wafer cones and sprinkles
The ice cream van stands firm, battery full
And we are powerless to resist the streams of strawberry sauce
So each white whippy ice cream cone
topped with a chocolate flake
Is brought to the car and passed over from soaking wet hands
To the soundtrack of otherworldly speech
Waves almost alive with determination
If we can't have treats when it's pouring
If we can't taste the flake crumbling now
When exactly can we?
Save us from waist deep puddles
With dopamine swirls
Let us sit, glued to our seats
Enjoying the bittersweetest of treats

little nightmares

Ghosts and foreshadows
Keep following me around
Some light and some dark
I want them to go away
And stay out of sight

Ghosts and foreshadows
Keep pulling at threads
Trying to unravel our lives
I want them to transform
And flood us with light

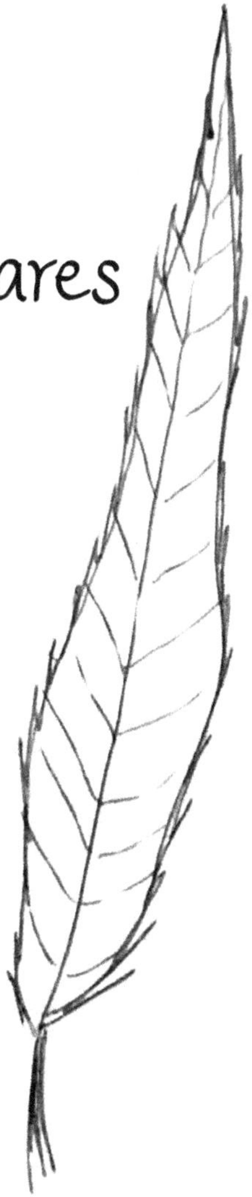

father

It's your day today
But do you deserve it?
Have you been there or did you run away?

It's your day today
You definitely show it
Have to make sure your effort is on display

It's your day today
But do you really need it?
Is it too complicated, is there too much to say?

It's your day today
You've truly earned it
You've been there every single day

It's your day today
But was your heart ever in it?
Your desire for fatherhood seems to have gone astray

It's your day today
You always try your best
Even when struggling, you pretend to be okay

tomorrow's song

Tomorrow's song blasts out
On the car radio
I am not ready
For these notes
Or that voice
The lyrics feel intrusive
But the volume dial won't turn
And the power button is broken
So the radio keeps playing
This music from the future
I tap my foot anyway
Unable to stop

from dust to dawn

We find calm and peace
In the lull, in the dark when
the winter lights glow

But the foreshadows
Of the tempest follow us
Wherever we go

carried

Your name drops out of the thoughts
And memories of other people
But our love for you remains constant
Your photos are everywhere
There will never be more
But we take photos for you all the time
Your life may be unknown to many
Just a sad echo on the wind
But we will carry you with us
Always

all day i will worry about you

You didn't go into school happy
And I could see the meltdown building
But I couldn't stay to calm you
The doors were already closed
So I just walked away
And now I will worry about you all day

After the thoughts play too freely on my mind
I'll email your teacher, who is too busy I know
But I keep imagining your sad little face
And your heart thumping
Just as I've replayed every scenario a hundred times
Your teacher will reply, don't worry he's fine
But I have to worry, after all, he's mine

summer snapshots

Sitting in the back garden, no rain, only a warm breeze, she could be my sister, our dark hair matches, but we're not even cousins. She bites into a ripe cherry tomato and seeds and guts fly at the speed of an unexpected sneeze and land on my top. I can't be older than about three but this is where my dislike of barbecues began.

Lying on the settee as evening was ready to jump out and push the day out of the way and I wake from a little sleep. In the garden-facing window I see bubbles floating like magic or fairies, just floating into things and bursting. Just a sprinkle of fairy dust.

Running between trees by ourselves. Tearing through the back lane on our bikes. Riding straight into a breezeblock wall — surely that was never there before? This is what comes of showing off. But I still just wanted them to like me.

A ghostly shroud covers us. The humidity of a landlocked state chokes us. In a house with two staircases with footsteps where there were no feet. We are caretakers of a home connected to a church by a single locked door. Dark and large. Too many rooms to keep checking. And too many spirits to keep ignoring. Feelings keep clinging on, dust and denial. Friendship is forged but will quickly be forgotten.

You can't have jacket potato and chips together, so scratch it off your order pad. The log cabin may let all the spiders in and you won't find Nessy no matter how hard you stare at the loch. That tartan skirt will never fit you.

The last remnants of the season are lingering on my forehead in unsure apprehension. I'm a 90s Welsh kid and this Canadian weather is super charged with newness. Saying hello to everyone, but realising no one wants to talk to me. But at least it's away, at least it's far, at least.

Hideaway in the in-between, watching *Beauty and the Beast* every day and spending all your money on ice cream from the video rental shop. But you have to go out as early as possible as there will be less people. This existence is clipped and confined by thoughts and walls.

Saltwater tangled hair. I'll save the biggest wave for later. Own rug pulled and changed, freer but still not right. A different wrong, where you tie a bow, but the ribbons keep facing the wrong way. Growth through error is manifesting. Feet keep walking along the promenade where the sea seems to go on forever. Pens scrape on paper, books pile up, but only topple when ignored.

Splashing my feet in the pools of the unknown. Irritation bubbling up like the hot tub I'll never go near. Life is on the cusp of becoming parental, but not just in the way I think. A body I had worked for is stretching, and the family I took comfort in is falling apart, a puncture lying under the facade. The condensation will drip down the non-alcoholic drink and I'll wish we hadn't spent the money to be there.

The rough sun is beating over the parched earth. My hair is sticking to the back of my neck and everyone looks so happy with their dinner alfresco and dresses and sandals, while topless men wander the pavements. I'm trying to make memories for them so they have something to say when the teachers ask on the first week back. But I'm desperately begging for rain, so I can ruin all this sunshine because this black hole of grief is drawing everything in and yet I feel like the only one to realise.

too afraid

I don't know how to explain this
But I'm afraid of absolutely everything
Things going badly, things going well
I feel like the weather in that moment
Where it could go either way
I would like to run, but I'm barely crawling through

My mind is caught in the split-second possibilities
Where one decision means fortune
The other pain
But because decisions are too big a step
I stay still and hope another crossroads appears
With only positive exits
I would like to walk, but I'm too busy shuffling my feet

I can't speak in case I say something stupid
And everyone thinks what's wrong with HER?
I don't want to go out on a limb
Because what if that bone snaps
And I end up in plaster
I feel the anticipation of fear rising even when I smile
I would like to skip, but I can't show that much happiness

In case it's taken away

just another dream

Everyone knows it's dull
hearing about other people's dreams
And this one is as dull as they come
Entirely normal, but not normal
I'm waiting in a queue at the post office
It's a normal queue but it's an abnormal queue
It's a weird gated queue on a small stage
I have a double buggy with me
with a baby and a toddler in it
One bald, one dark and cuddled together
Two boys
And I start an argument because I refuse to wait anymore
I jump the barrier and go
And the double buggy is somehow now a shopping trolley
Yet this is totally normal
But they are still there. Two boys
One bald, one dark and cuddled together
And I'm still arguing
Because apparently I was meant to stay in the queue
An apparently normal thing to do
And I wake up thinking about the buggy
About the shopping trolley
And I realise the baby was my youngest
and the toddler was his brother

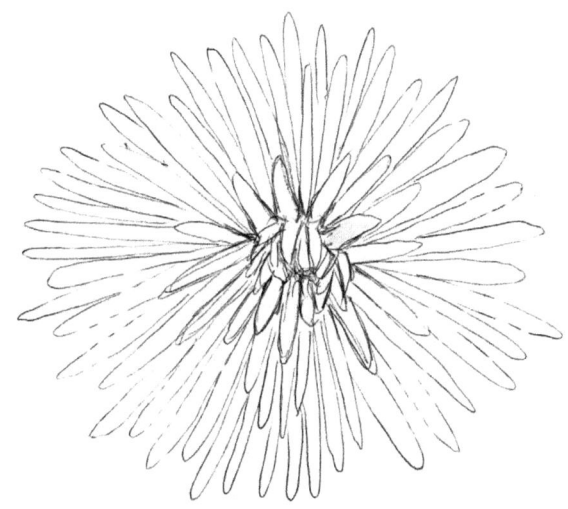

Who he never met
As he died
And in all the stupidness of the argument
Of the gated queue
He was there, like it was normal
Just sitting with his younger brother
Just there in the abnormal but normal of dream life
And it was nice to be with him
Even if it wasn't real
And next time I lie down to sleep
Perhaps I'll see him again
In the normal but abnormal normal of dreams
And I'll get to drive along with a car not missing a car seat
Except it won't be a car it'll be a boat with wheels
Or I'll get to go shopping and push the double buggy around
Except it won't be a buggy it'll be a wheelbarrow
But it'll seem totally normal
So normal

anemoia

I'm nostalgic for places I've never been

Those magnificent old world cities and ancient forests and rolling landscapes, trains that billow steam and carry me to a castle to learn more than sums, aromatic coffee shops calling me in, books in brown bags and the smell of the freshest air ungraspable in my hands, and the sands of shores falling between each finger as I watch the horizon in awe and the snow falls and gathers in all the right places

For lives I've never lived

A large inner city family cushioning me on my return home from the office, cutting chunks of butter to be smeared on freshly made bread in the farmhouse kitchen, jokes boisterous and tales dripping their way through the generations, universities with stirring architecture, where I walk with cap and gown, effortless and smiling, headed straight for the chance of a lifetime before I was even born

For houses I've never seen

Only online or in my imagination, with grey stone symmetry and a green view, where an open fire warms the cold deep down in my soul and the rain spatters the light bearing windows that frame the garden that seems to go on for miles, the old flat, compact and cosy with the city view that flows in through the living room windows and thousands and thousands of fairy lights cut through any darkness

For people I don't know

The ones I swear could be my best friends if we only knew each other better, or ones I've never even met, that my mind has made up on a lonely hour, people that surround me with joy, where people seek me out, where family grew like the biggest tree and I'm nestled on a branch supported by the strongest foundations and inside jokes you could paper the walls with and people that show up with food prepared exactly when you need it

And for feelings I've only felt in dreams

Wholeness, completeness and peace, where I hold each child of mine close, where all their hearts beat and their chests rise and fall with ease, where happiness isn't frightening, love is everything and sadness is only fleeting idea, fear is a momentary blip, where it feels okay to just be me and we are free, freer than birds and more comfortable than the best winter jumper could ever be

rebuilding

Words are flying through the air
Like the Red Arrows but less orderly
More like a jumble sale

Knitted gloves are being purchased
Because little hands are freezing in autumn air
Quickly abandoned to crunch leaves with bare fingers

Frustration is swelling in our middles
Radiating up and out
Crumbling paper, throwing it angrily into the bin

Words are being carved through wet sand
Slower, but not quite snail pace
Shells are being placed around the letters

Little windmills are being perused
Hands are turning their sails on a still day
The sticks will be pushed into the soil and left

Sadness is building behind our eyes
Reaching the top of the waterfall
Flowing out, tumbling down stream

Words are spilling over cups and saucers
Cake is being gobbled down
Crumbs pushed onto side plates or raining like snow

Hands are tapping on windowpanes
Ready to leave, to grasp the chains of the swings
Whoosh, feet first, thoughts second

Joy is dwelling in the foundations
Growing through the soil, evergreen
Smiling with the light, beaming down on each face

not the same

Our stories are not
The same so we don't have to
Tell them like they are

Our lives are not
The same so we don't have to
Live them like they are

Our thoughts are not
The same so we don't have to
Think them like they are

panic

Silver hills
Not from frost or a light dusting of snow
but fog that continues its descent
Like shadows of the past still lingering
With the wind pushing its cries through the gap
under the door
Rattling, almost as if you're knocking to come in
I'm not sure if the bolts I slid across will keep you out
I'm not sure I want them to
This morning is clogged with ghosts
And there is no light from fires
There is only panic

miles in memory

Intentional steps add up to miles in remembrance
Footsteps like heartbeats across grass or gravel or tarmac
Memories surface through trees
Tears get washed away along the shore
Anger gets stamped on pavement slabs
Purpose is never forgotten
And thoughts are focused on all those souls
Gone too soon

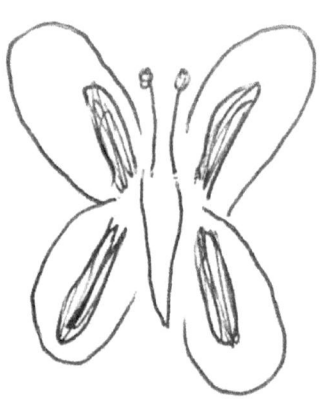

unread letters

They might look like unread letters
But each word that's written is seen
By hearts, minds and souls
On Earth and on the Other Side
So writing to you is never a waste of time
It is always with love and with hope
A special way to hold you close

summer solstice

The summer sun shines
Midway through another year
So life can be bright

And all the souls can
Can share their many stories
Of wonder and light

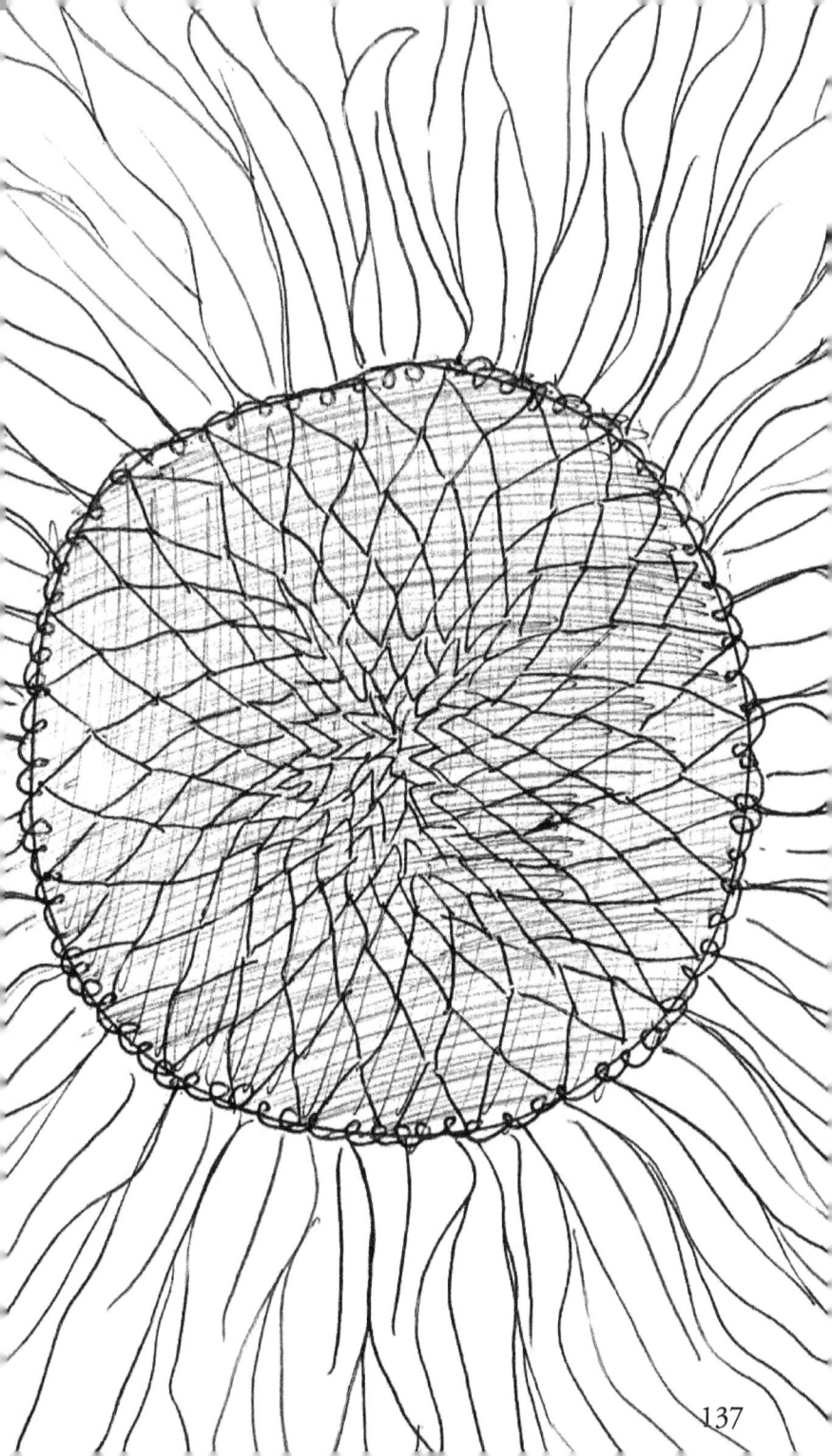

birthday presents

I could wrap up all the presents in the world
In the prettiest paper
But none of them would ever do
Because none of them would be you

I can't ask heaven to send you to me
Because I don't have a direct line
I can only hope for little signs from you
To let me know you miss me too

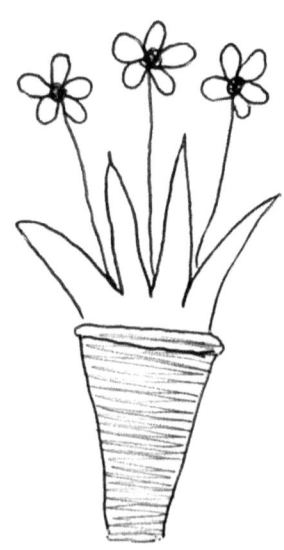

ink stains

My hand is covered
Stained from the words I scribbled
Over and over

To purge my mind of
The thoughts running wild and loud
Yet more words turn up

Spinning round and round
Demanding to be written
In permanent ink

yellow roses

A single yellow rose
Grows in the midst of green stems and leaves
With sharp thorns ready to protect its beauty
It drinks all the rain offers
And soaks up the sun rays
Lonely but grateful for the chance to bloom
One by one the petals will start to droop
Then fall, drifting to the soil below
To offer some goodness in repayment
Asking again for the chance to grow

brooding

Grey skies form above
The masked moon plagues all the stars
Dust begins to fall
Earth's foreboding clouds brood
Ready to rain down starlight

there we go then

There go our ghosts
Lingering in rooms we left long ago
Repeating the same phone calls
Speaking the same words over
and over

There go our echoes
Swimming around in the sea
Digging our imprints into the sand
Picking up shells and rocks over
and over

There go our shadows
Walking through the trees
Tripping over protruding roots
Telling the same stories over
and over

river

The flow of my thoughts drips down and down
Over old stones and newer tree branches
Some words drown
Others bounce onto the bank
Either way I hope never to see them again
And some words go round and round
Caught in a little whirlpool
Where the ideas flow fast
And I feel dizzy and nauseated
Then skimming stone memories ripple smiles
Which fade or brighten if the sky allows
Other thoughts get stuck on errant rubbish that's been dumped
Shouting, trying to make themselves known
The majority keep going
Flowing away, unnoticed and untroubled
Headed to join the sea's constant chatter
And the select few rise up to the clouds
Stretching out in the grey
Before raining themselves back down
Over and over again

blustery day

In midsummer I long for a blustery day
To feel that little shiver up my spine
To grab the cosiest jumper to warm up
To watch the leaves fly past or stick to the pavement
To see raindrops land on my head or windowpane
To watch the last remnants of summer giveaway to the richness of autumn
And to fall into the season with delight

moonstone

Did the moon encapsulate a piece of its energy
Within you

Did the light that flowed through your layers
Imbibe you

Did the waves that washed you up on the shore
Release you

Did the hands that held you close to their heart
Know you

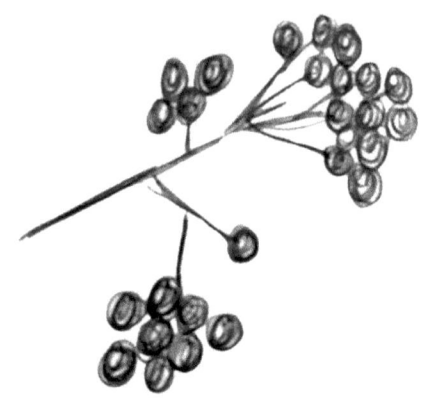

name tag

After I was born and my mum went back
to the postnatal ward
All the other mums called their babies Danielle
Every single one
My name was a dinosaur name, very old fashioned
But if it was good enough for the queen, then it was good enough for me, right?
And as I grew there was always a Danielle about
But it was never me
I was always on the outside looking in
Or on the outside trying to set it all ablaze
When I got my first job in a high street clothes shop
The manager kept calling me Danielle
No one knew why

I even had to wear a Danielle name tag
Because they had so many spare
I guess there were so many Danielles my age
I must be one too
But it didn't make me suddenly fit in
Although for a time I thought I might
Glide across my new identity
Finally I'm Danielle
But I wasn't
And really everyone could tell
That I would never be
A Danielle

sand dune

The sand gets everywhere
In socks, under fingernails
In the pockets of my handbag
I'm forced to carry it around
Until it starts to seep out
And I leave a trail of it
Wherever I go

camera

You don't like having your photo taken
So you always pull an awkward face
Because you like to smile at people not a black box
Or the back of a smartphone
But you're not smiling at an inanimate object
Not really
You're looking at the future
And the people that will look back and see you
As you are now
And your face will pull at their heartstrings
with that familiar bittersweetness
And they'll smile to themselves and think,
oh they hated having their photo taken
And suddenly they'll peruse their memories
like a slideshow in their mind
And say oh
I wish they were here

magic spell

If magic was real
I would say spell after spell
To fix all of the wrongs
So that we could never tell

I can't wave a wand
And send all the pain away
But I wish someone would
More than I could ever say

change my mind

Go on, change my mind
I'm not a fixed point, not stuck
Happy to hear you
Happy to know more and more
I'm glad for the chance to grow

dog days

I'm calling you off for rain
I'm telling everyone to go home
This party is over and I am not sad about it
I'm furious that you all want so much
That you try to get things
That never were meant for you
That you want more and more
Clinging on to cutlery and tablecloths
As I push you out the door
I'm telling you to not come back
And I'm paying the bill with sweat building
On my furrowed brow, full of panic and lack
The dog days humidity deepening discomfort
Your greedy faces won't be allowed back
I'm hanging on for the dead of winter
When the guest list will be shorter and new
And because if you're name's not down
Then summer won't release you

car radio

Your song keeps playing
On the car radio
And whenever the opening notes begin
I breathe that little bit quicker
As it feels like you've somehow sent
Yourself down to me through the waves
And I wish I could listen on repeat
Even if the words lose all meaning

water lily

In the dead of night your petals are tightly closed
Ready to open up with the sun and drink it all in
Each new day another chance to grow
An opportunity to start again
A daily resurrection

curtain twitcher

It's hard to not peep at the side of curtains
When three police vans and six officers
Come to search your neighbour's house
It's hard to mind your own business
When your neighbour's marriage breaks down
On the street in front of your door
It's hard to look the other way
When your neighbour lets her very young children roam the streets unsupervised
It's hard to not peer through the blinds
When that woman is walking past with her dog again
It's hard to not sneak a glance in your neighbour's garden
When the noise has been going on all night
It's hard not to keep looking across the road
When all those cars have been coming and going
It's hard to not feel utterly alone
When we all live in isolation

potholes

When they said it was going to be a bumpy ride
I didn't think they meant like this
I didn't expect the ups and downs to be so sudden
For cancellations to flash up at the last minute
Or doors to be unlockable
For healing to be at the bottom of the list
Because there's just so much to do
I didn't expect puddles of rain to gather
In the gaps I hadn't filled
Or lightbulbs to flash with misfortune rather than ideas
I thought there may be a reprieve somewhere along the way
But even if there was I might miss it
Because I am too focused on the potholes

ruby

Can you bring me love
Gather it up and wrap it
Ready for planting

Soil will help it thrive
And there'll be rubies and gold
In the flowerbeds

We can pick our blooms
Throw them up into the sky
Leave the rest to grow

The love you brought me
Will spread all over the world
Propagating light

smile, it might never happen

In the rolls of thunder
You should smile more
In the torrential rain
You should smile more
In the sunburnt heatwave
You should smile more
In the frozen snowdrift
You should smile more
In the heart of the tornado
You should smile more

sunglasses

The sun got in your eyes
Through the pouring rain
The waves rolled over your feet
But you refused to find shade
You dug your heels into wet sand
And waited for the sun to set
You tried to hear the sea's message
And wrote your reply with pebbles
You stood there until the sun rose
With your face bare to the sky
**Refusing to live in the shadow
Of then and now, hello and goodbye**

childhood stories

There you are telling tales again
Those stories of truth and lies
Trying to get the attention you need
Fed up of hearing your own cries

Trying to be someone else, someone better
Frustrated with both the sun and the moon
The sky and its clouds that insist on passing by
Alarmed that things keep happening too soon

But you'll say those stories again and again
The ones you've rewritten, you'll retell
Because imagination is a safer place
One where all tales can dwell

When nobody wants to hold your hand
You'll count each star in the night sky
Replaying imagined **futures** and rewritten pasts
Without **even questioning** why

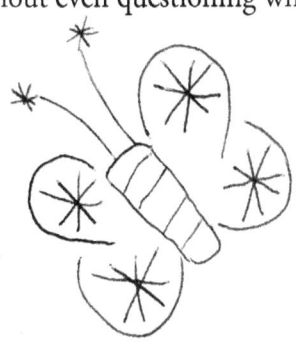

blackbird

Under the morning sky
A blackbird calls
From the top of a silver birch tree
He's tearing up the alphabet
And moving letters
Arranging them in a line
He swoops down
Carrying the words on his wings
He shakes them off onto the ground
And hurriedly buries them in the earth
All of the syllables
All of the meaning
Every sentence lost
Up and up he flies
Sweetly singing truth and lies

all the birds

There's a bird sitting on a branch of your tree
This morning as I watch the sun rise in the sky
I like to think all the birds are you
Of course I know they can't all be you
But let me indulge that certain ones are
And you've come to see me for a moment
To bring me a piece of heaven
That I can carry with me all day long

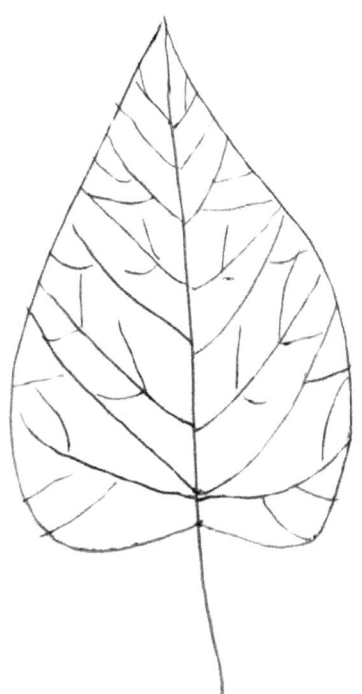

ghosts from the waves

They walked out of the waves
Displaced and confused
Hailing taxis and dropping water all over the backseat, asking for long journeys with no money to pay
And then gone

They rang doorbells and silently asked for help
They were wrapped in towels and offered warm drinks
Unable to say why they were there or where they'd been
And then gone

They stood by familiar homes, workplace entrances, shops
Looking for someone or something they knew
Waiting patiently in the rain when no rain fell
And then gone

They saw the water rise and cover everything like a blanket
But without the comfort
How it pulled underripe fruit from hanging branches while waves snatched at it greedily
And then gone

They just needed to be directed to the light
The sunrise
The fluorescent
The moonshine
The unapproachable
The candle glow

And then

Gone

all too well

I'm not sure who days like today are for
Because bereaved parents are aware
with every breath they take
That their child no longer breathes, or never did
And I know the point is to bring awareness
to those who don't know
Who don't understand
And to remind people that our children matter
and always will
But is it just another day amongst the noise
Another post to quickly scroll past
Another thing to be pushed away
I don't know
But I hope there are people who care,
people willing to learn and share
To help keep memories breathing
And I know I'll be here
With a candle lit, sending love to everyone
All of us who are all too aware

summer lies

It is not quite Friday and I am more tired than the moon
The summer keeps telling lies
Offering sandcastles and sundaes
And then snatching them away on Saturday mornings
Smugger than the greyest Monday clouds
Wednesday is holding out hope, it could go either way
Sunday has all but given up,
offering the rest but so few take it up
The blue sky lingers a bit on Thursday
But Tuesday is the worst of all
The disappointment of another failed week hits already
And the promise of holiday sunshine remains hidden
amongst the dandelions
Where nobody thought to look

confetti

Falling petals flow
Through the air as confetti
Drifting like snowflakes
Before raining down on us
With otherworldly blessings

still

Maybe you didn't get what you wanted
Yet the sunflowers seeds still grow
Maybe you got what you wanted
And birds still fly through the sky
Maybe hope feels lost
Yet the sun still rises
Maybe hope is in abundance
And the stars in the night sky still glow

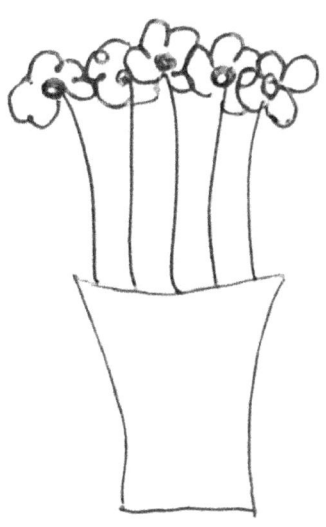

grief cake

The recipe for this cake has been developed over many years and yet in many ways it hasn't changed at all. It still feels like lead in the pit of your stomach and leaves a bittersweet taste on the tongue. But people must take bites regardless and swallow them down, choke slightly as if it were gravel, and then wait for it to regurgitate a bit, before sinking and sinking and sinking.

ingredients

200g various pain
200g shock
4 x desperation
200g memories and imagined futures
1 tsp replaying, endless replaying
2 tbsp tears

method
(order irrelevant)

Step 1: Preheat your body, mind and soul to 180 degrees along with the oven.

Step 2: Break the desperation into the bowl and pray, beg and plead for none of this to be true.

Step 3: Mix in the various pain, likely from the heart, stomach and head, but whatever you have inside will work.

Step 4: Fold in the shock - don't worry if the mixture looks numb at this point.

Step 5: Let tear-inducing memories and lost futures drip down and decorate the mix with devastation.

Step 6: Replay moments of sudden news, of phone calls, of doctors, of goodbyes, of ashes, of freshly dug soil, of laboured breaths, of petals and green stems, of coldness, of stillness over and over again.

Step 7: Pour everything into tins, place in the centre of the oven and your mind, heart and soul and allow mixture to bake into a cake.

Step 8: Eat immediately, do your best to swallow each piece and realise none of this is going to get any better and you'll have to keep making and eating this cake every day, but you'll eventually grow accustomed to its taste and texture.

Please note — gritty crumbs will spill out of your mouth no matter how hard you try to keep them in. Be aware that no one will say anything about this as it's too awkward.

the afterthought

The sun rises up over another new place
Sleep plagues the eyes of a youthful face
Another town, another village,
another city, another school
Another opportunity to feel like a fool
The trouble with always being the new kid
on the street
Is never forging true connections
with anyone you meet
Never picked first, never liked first, never invited first
Existing on the peripheries, dwelling in the liminal,
learning to expect the worst
You're always soon gone, soon forgotten, soon moving,
but free to roam
You can always talk to your old friends on the phone
And always saying yes I'm okay, yes I'm fine
Yes the experience is fantastic, I'm having a great time
But really it's miserable to feel all alone
Especially when nowhere feels like home

extraordinary

Babies are little miracles
Sent to us as blessings
Wonderful sparks of light
Full of glinting magic
And extraordinary delight

a song of self-sabotage

I wander by the ocean's edge
To seek out a little bit more than solitude
Watching as the water whirls; it overwhelms then retreats
Dragging back everything I want to hold onto
And I'm singing a song of self-sabotage
Watching the sea and the pebbles wage war
Searching for ghosts in my mind
While waiting for a moment to emerge
Perhaps a little wisp of magic or a full-bodied apparition
From sand or sea or sky or shell or sonnet
But all I hear is distant whispering
Both ancient and immediate in tone
I'm looking for all the messages
that are just beyond my reach
Watching as the sea throws each one in the air
before snatching it back
Lost amongst the splash and crash of waves that have been
around forever
And I keep singing my song of self-sabotage
Watching the ghosts of the past, present and future dance
around my brain
Until the tide gets fed up and pushes me away

no balm can fix this

Healing from summer's secrets awaits
We're living low while the sun is high
Applying sun cream like a medicinal balm
Heart and soul more in need than our faces

The door knocks and it keeps knocking
Peace is being stolen piece by piece
Being pulled inch by inch under the doorframe
The damage has been done here

The edge of tears balances and unbalances at whim
Oh that song is playing again
Oh that feather is falling again
The grave is full with fresh flowers

The weather app is broken from overuse
Surely it must be time for rain
Never mind, I'll water the driest summer for years
With the tidal waves of grief

take this test to rewrite time

At 16:09 on a crisp January day were you
A. At home drinking Chardonnay
B. Counting the lines on the last of the fallen leaves
C. Holding the dying body of your newly born son
D. Packing up a picnic to eat in a snowdrift

In a council building midweek in early February did you
A. Turn up and shout at the employees about your council tax bill with red rage ravaging
B. Register your baby's birth with a special joy and smile, leaving the smell of milk and nappy cream lingering
C. Register your baby's birth and death and leave with only paper in your hands
D. Leave the buds of snowdrops and daffodils as an offering to each passing ghost

On the day after Valentine's Day did the rain

A. Flood the stream at the bottom of the garden

B. Seep through holes in your umbrella

C. Hit the soil at the bottom of his freshly dug grave

D. Make puddles for newly purchased wellington boots to splash in

On an afternoon, just before the week became weekend, one revolution later, did the branches of the tree

A. Grow unexpected green leaves

B. Fall across the road, stopping traffic for hours

C. Become decorated with seed imbibed heart-shaped paper as a memorial to all the children gone too soon

D. Get chopped off. They were rotten to the core

Why is it, every time you take this test, the answer is always C?

unpicking

I tied it all up together
But not with a bow
No ribbon or floral garland
I used old twine that had faded with age
And I knotted it so tightly my fingers bled

Now the only way to unpack these things
Would be to pick away slowly
Nails worn down to the skin
Because a snip from the shortcut scissors
Somehow ties the twine even tighter

do you?

Do you ever feel like a spinning top
Spinning so fast that you just can't stop

Do you ever feel like a ball of rage
Rolling around in a metal cage

Do you ever feeling like a monster truck
Crashing around, covered in muck

Do you ever feel like a bird in the sky
Flapping your wings without knowing why

Do you ever feeling like a racing car
Driving around yet never going far

Do you ever feel like a homemade kite
Even with the wind at your back you just can't take flight

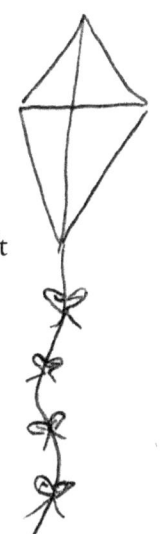

uncountable stars

I could count the stars
In the spectacular night sky
And write each number down
But it would never add up to
Exactly how much I miss you

how do we stop it?

When the morning dawns with disbelief
The horror screams of mothers can still be heard
Carried on the air that flows across the whole world
Even though the new day arrives with silence

Fear has been released on the innocent
Lives that should be bright have been forced to fade away
Blood stains will never be cleaned
They'll be imprinted onto minds, into skin like tattoos

Mothers, fathers, family, friends, and people
who were unconnected but suddenly intrinsically linked
Now looking on helplessly
Angry, frustrated and broken
With guttural, uncontrollable, unbreathable tears

This devastation will not be contained
It will drip into the water supply
And we will all drink it
Whether we know it or not

Because this evil keeps tearing at the heart of our love
But we don't know how to stop it

hand of god

He told me that ever since his 87th birthday
He'd felt the hand of God on him
Like he was being pulled away from this material world
And was becoming more and more aware
of his earthly body's deterioration
The light shining brighter every day
Just outside his peripheral vision
Asking everyone how they are
Is becoming tiresome, he explained
Analysing if today is a good day or bad
Is like an ongoing sigh
And night keeps drawing in
Faster each day, as time spins on
And he said he thought we live too long
My heart felt like this was true and false all at once
Like I had just heard the best and most terrible lullaby
But the whispers on the wind said
God knows what he's doing
Even when we do not

longing

The morning is grey
The sea is lost to the mist
The waves long for rain

The morning is cold
The trees are lost to the clouds
The leaves long for sun

The morning is humid
The stone is lost to haze
The ground longs for snow

photographs of still life

My camera roll is life punctuated by death
Flowers for a memorial, full bloom or emerging
Petals just drifting, just like snowflakes falling
Smiles on a child, maybe forced or real
Running across a park, playing games,
maybe laughing with delight or standing together quickly,
irked by the interruption
A freshly wiped gravestone
With a slight reflection of the sky above it
While the seagulls squawk from miles away
A freshly baked cake iced with bittersweetness
Slices cut bigger than anyone can stomach
Forests of green or beaches of gold with red hair and blond
Billowing across the image
The echoes of squeals almost heard
Weeds and grass trying to make their way under the border
Echoes of blinding tears and sobs
Dance across the decorative pebbles
Photographs of still life go on and on and on
Life and death merge in every album, on every image

let's talk it out

Light cuts through the dark
But the shadows still linger
Candle light flickers, but doesn't extinguish
Frost gathers, but refuses to clear
But the blankets are warm
And your embrace is soothing
Love cuts through the desolation
And the healing trickles through

growing with his echo

I like to think of you growing with his echo
Both housed in the same small home
Hands held, ghost to flesh
Souls meeting but then parting for now
Because it's a special thing to follow on
To bring life after death
I think of you sitting in his imprints
Like an old armchair
As if it held you both together
While taking time to develop in the darkroom
With the twinkling light of his love still there
I don't know if you'll ever remember his echo
Maybe just a warm feeling that fleetingly grasps your core
Or a sound or sight that's just out of reach
Through everything you do
As the eternal light will always reflect within you

growth

I wrote your story
On the lines of every leaf
The words echo through
All the trees in the forest
But only grow in my dreams

nausea

Sometimes when I think of the past
I'm choked
But not with nostalgia
By nausea
Things that used to be nice memories
Suddenly start turning my stomach
And I'm never exactly sure why
Maybe it's just the passing of time
And the years that have elapsed
Highlight all the things I thought I'd do
But haven't
Or maybe I can't help but look back and taint everything
Because I expect everything to have a sting in the tail
Hidden somewhere

if

The hangman is in the light fitting
Hiding amongst the dark shadows
If the light would just flick on
It would all disappear

The three piece suite is out in the rain
None of it is water tight
If the sun would just come out
It would all dry up

The reflection is in the mirror
But eyes are shut tightly
If deep breaths could be taken
It would all become clear

The ghost is out by the shore
Bobbing with each wave
If one person should turn their head
It would all flood

calling your name

I like to think that when a name is written in the sand
They are called to you
So wherever you are in the world
From the local beach to far away sands
Their spirit will stand beside you
Taking in a scene they were denied in life
So every time a name is written
You forge a deeper connection
Between life and all that we cannot see

phoenix dactylifera

I've seen you growing via photos and text
On posts not directly for me
Through a screen of limited reality
I only knew you in physical proximity for a year or so
And I saw your wedding photos twice
Never asking what happened in between
But you grew to the height of a small palm tree
Not knowing the dates you bloomed would provide more than sustenance
A count up or down, whichever way you prefer to look
With palms slowly drooping
A rot in a branch slowly spreading through
And watching from afar as announcements of joy turn to announcements of pain
With so many replies saying you'll beat this, you will
You'll rise from the ashes
And for so many years the palms bloom and subside
From green to grey
But with dates no longer growing
And an eternal tiredness beating at your core
Inviting the whole of Facebook to your living wake
Again watching wordless and feeling like an intruder
Nervous for the day someone else posts
To say the phoenix has stopped rising

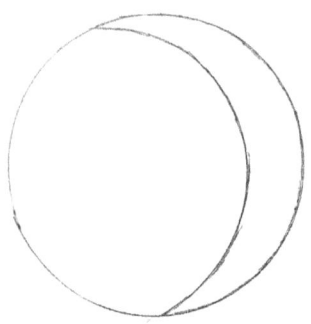

the moon, august 2024

As red as the moon on August 18th
Reflecting the burning in our cores
The clouds won't hide you
While the wildfire still roars

As blue as the moon on August 19th
Reflecting the raindrops on the sea
The clouds will fall around you
While the nightingales fly free

As grey as the moon on August 20th
Reflecting the echoes in stone
The clouds will pass by you
While the words remain unknown

seeing differently

The trees I planted or encouraged
are slowly changing our view
Small trunks I pulled out from chicken wire
Or saplings I plonked in the ground with no real clue
Leaves acting like net curtains to passers by
Making us focus between gaps to see any blue
Reaching as if they were on tiptoes, trying to touch the sky
Fully green in the finest peacock bloom
Dressed with sunrise summer dew
And even if the growth is slow I am trying
To reach with the branches and break through

body clock

Winter beckons
And for once I am fearful for its approach
Because another winter
Is another year
And another year
Means more behind
Than ahead
Maybe
Or perhaps I haven't yet got halfway
It's impossible to know
But I am growing not just older
But more disillusioned
And more desperate
For something I can't quite put my finger on
But I feel it
And ignore it
Yet it churns in my stomach
And nags at my thoughts
Yet I still seem to be waiting
For this unattainable feeling
Will I ever have enough time
To satisfy it?

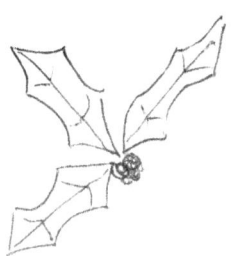

ready for winter

Winter gestures with open hand
Which I'll clasp tightly within mine
Let it pull me into the dark nights and twinkling lights
To where the frost gathers in memories like decoration
And I won't need to worry about my fringe
sticking to my forehead
But whether the wind has messed it up instead
As we kick leaves and watch as they fall to the ground
like the slowest snowflakes
And I light imaginary fires in the grate that doesn't exist
in my living room
While I relish putting on jumpers
and grabbing a scarf before walking out the door
Or watch wrapping paper be ripped
and land to the floor like confetti
While familiar stories play out on screen or paper
With snowdrops starting to burst through the cold ground
And warm drinks warm hands and faces
I'll dwell on these moments over and over
Even though the leaves are yet to fall

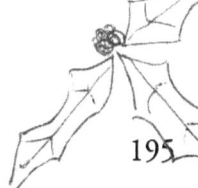

broken record

Winter calls and my shoulders sag with heaviness
Because another winter completes another year
Without him
It means the Earth has completed another revolution
And we are still living with a piece missing
Where sadness and happiness flow together
Like water and salt in the sea
And to others we may seem like a broken record
But we are broken and we have no choice but to repeat
Because a short life only gets the chance
to make so many memories
And it is up to us to remember them

mixed narcissi

I handed over £5 in exchange for a bag of bulbs
Chosen on a quick supermarket visit
Because winter approaches
And I want to know there'll be colour
For you, come spring

And I want to know that life still blooms
Where your bones lie
So that when the new season emerges
Your grave will be as beautiful
As you were in life and your soul is in death

sunflower summer

I grew you from seed
Pushed you down into dark soil
Ready for you to emerge into light
Bright and beautiful and full of life
But a storm changed your path
And while your green stems grew
Your petals struggled
Though you were no less beautiful
And love emerged from every molecule
Every speck of stardust
As flowering was just beyond your reach
We will water our souls and bathe in sunlight
We will bloom for you

the words are on fire

They burn your letters
Thinking nobody cares
The paper slowly becoming ash
But the words can't be burned
The words join the air and fly
They're carried across the sky
And whisper along each breath of wind
If we could only be quiet
We might hear them

Not sorry

The wildflower grows
Unapologetic and free
Sharing joy and beauty

the sea's spell

In the lull, in the pause, you can hear the sea sing
Sometimes songs of sadness, sometimes of joy
And when the sun sparkles on the water it's like faeries dancing, with a hop and a spring
Waves hailing in a warning or blessing with the splash and crash and gentle sway
Accompanied by the rougher rustling of the sandbank brambles followed by their sting

But there's an excavator dredging the sand
And someone's painting a wall and listening to music through tinny speakers
Some long-forgotten 90s band
And people keep talking about the news or their neighbour, something about the prime minister, something about the weather, moaning that there's no seats and now they'll have to stand

They don't know they are breaking the sea's spell
As it surges and retreats along the shoreline, in the shadow of a castle, long ruined
Where only ghosts and birds now dwell
Even those birds swoop down to drown out the sound
Of the song of the sea, of the stories it might tell

gryffindor

Fire bright leaves warm my soul
As they drift from tired branches
To grace the ground below
And we walk through
Leaves crunching, being kicked up and forward
The wind nipping slightly
While the last hurrah of summer tries to cling on
And I see how wonderful it is to be here
As she laughs and runs and tells me silly stories
Her fiery coloured hair
mirroring the beauty of the changing season
The sky is starting to change, the wind is telling us it's time
And the leaves remain busy
laying out their path for transformation

Jessica

Gosh, I thought that was Jessica
She says, looking at me like I should know who Jessica is
And know that we look alike
As the first winds of autumn blow the salty air
through my hair
And all I can do is squint and half smile,
suddenly half-masked by the dark strands
Wondering who is Jessica
And why we look so alike

Are we both fat?
Do we both push a pram?
Do we share the same very dark brown hair?
With a fringe that the breeze has overtaken
Are both our faces lined with the heartache of grief?
Could we be the Sweet Valley Twins of our town?
Jessica and Elizabeth
I'm the studious one

Or is she the better version of me
The one who always remembers night cream
Who could commit to a career and stick to it
Who never troubled herself with words and images
running through her head
And didn't have any fillings in her teeth

Did the woman mutter to her friend when I walked away,
Although Jessica is prettier
Thinner
Wears just the right amount of makeup
Dresses better
Looks happier
Looks younger

Who is Jessica?
And do we really look alike?

float

Walking through the woods
With a hand poised to grasp
Pulling all the green off all the trees
Storing in palms for later
For when the fresh air has been left behind
Where the walls are up, doors locked, windows shut
Where the taps have been left on
And the water is rising, not just like the tide
Ankle deep, making its way to calf level
We will sink like stones
Joining the ghosts at the bottom
While the water keeps flowing
Only the green will float

chaos unleashed

Words and words tumble
This is now chaos, unleashed chaos
On paper, on screens
They want replies and comments
I am tired of answering

post migraine euphoria

Did she go to sleep with a smile on her face
A dream in her head and plan in place

Did she go to bed with tears in her eyes
Thoughts muddled up in falsehoods and lies

Did she go to bed as quiet as a mouse
Desperate to get away from her cursed house

Did she go to bed like an old beach stone
Tired and weary, with a gripe and a moan

Did she go to bed as light as a feather
Sun-kissed from the unseasonable weather

Did she go to bed with her face in a frown
Tossing and turning, despondent and down

Did she go to bed terribly afraid
Thinking of all the times she hadn't prayed

Did she go to bed with thoughts like a runaway train
Were things going to change or was it all going to repeat again

dark waters

Heavy, deep and cold
Ghosts of the dark waters flow
Translucent yet full
They call to you, they whisper
They hide your secrets below

happy heavenly birthday
to tom

Some may find it strange that we still celebrate
your birthday
But it is our special way of holding you close
Because there's so much we wish we could say
You're with us in everything we do
In quiet moments and in loud
We will always remember you
We look for whispers of you all day long
From the sunlight reflections on the sea
to the early morning robin's song
So when we smile with tears and say happy birthday
in the candlelit glow
We want you to see
That we love and miss you
more than anyone could know

14th january 2022

You didn't die today
But the countdown to your life
Became the countdown to your death
The sea and the sky will drain their colour
The green shoots waiting below ground will stop
And you'll keep moving, so unaware
So blissful and shut off to the pain
outside your water-filled home
The reservoir of tears won't make the world fertile enough
for you
No matter how many pleading prayers I say
Wishing life where life cannot stay
The water is going to drain and swirl away
You'll breathe and stop
And up and up you'll fly
My heart in the stars
The brightest light in the sky

messages from heaven

The trees are full of otherworldly blossom
The kind that only shows up when branches are bare
The sky is thick with possibility
Wings are cutting through the air
The robins are bringing their messages
Their beaks are crammed full of words
Heaven is busy sending letters
But only the persistent can be heard

get over it

So terribly sad
Stop going on about it
You've got other kids

But why should I forget one
I'm still the mother of you

Get over it now
Please stop dwelling on the past
Why are you still sad

I don't mind ruminating
If I can stay close to you

Move on now, they say
Focus on other things, okay?
But I don't want to

I am happy to remain
Haunted by the ghost of you

october

Orange leaves fall down
The evergreen watch over
Loss pulls at their stems

Cobwebs decorate
Those bare branches like tinsel
Autumn sun shines through

Earthly magic dwells
It takes back to give again
Waiting below ground

Fallen foliage
Is now gathered for winter
We must prepare warmth

The black cat hisses
Tired of all the symbolism
Wants to just be here

Jokes aren't welcome now
Not now that the air has turned
Frost nips all it holds

But warmth builds inside
The heart of home is aglow
Cosy moments flow

Longing is reaching
New heights in our souls and hearts
For those gone too soon

Pulling at our thoughts
Unanswered questions swirl yet
Nature does not mind

The brisk walk goes on
It takes it all in its stride
Until heads are clear

The rustle of leaves
Whispering the words again
They cling to branches

The ghosts are quiet
They don't need to cause a fuss
Lingering softly

The autumn beauty
Distracts even the busy
Lost amongst the flow

So tired but not quite
Ready for hibernation
It's time to slow down

No spells are wanted
We don't need a love potion
To grasp the season

Building homes in fog
Not all our green fades away
More than leaves may fall

Ghosts might be waiting
Getting ready for haunting
But some just live here

Hiding in the dark
The emerging frost lies down
Hoping for grey skies

Don't ignite the flames
The roaring fire won't last
Wind won't take the ash

The witch's hat won't
Fly through the dark sky tonight
The rain will stop play

Big drops will fall down
The rain storm will flood us all
It will cleanse us too

The fallen leaves will
Float across every puddle
Colourful and cold

But at least the frost
Won't bite us while the rain falls
It falls and it falls

The darkening skies
Still want to draw out the night
The stars want more time

Yet another chance
To sparkle, so light, so bright
So welcome tonight

Light will cut through dark
Will provide a way back home
Even through the cloud

Skies are not dreary
The mist from the dragon's breath
Dissipates slowly

Morning dawns again
Across orange pumpkin fields
Almost too ripe now

Dying embers lie
Birds feast on nature's decay
Time to fly away

The veil hangs thin now
Here and there are bedfellows
Candle light flickers

Yet light overwhelms
The saints are praying for us
Time to start again

dear autumn sky

Your veil has been lifted
Opening us up to what lies beyond
Letting in the vast blue hue
Your vibrancy deepened by the yellow and red trees
That have given up the ghost
The moon is moving closer to earth to borrow their earthy tones
And the sun is sitting lower
In an attempt to focus our eyes on light
In a season ready for darkness
Where your night is bursting with clusters of stars
Providing a different view on infinity

interruption

As I sat with the TV on
Same old programmes, same old new episodes
Baby in the crook of my arm sleeping peacefully
A hearse and mourners cars drive past my window
And I could see the coffin through the glass
And I thought
Here I am being utterly normal, maybe boring
And people are passing me by
In the worst times of their lives
And when I was in the worst time of my life
Looking at a very small coffin
Other people were in their houses
Making cups of tea
Eating a cake
Watching TV
Having a nap
Doing the washing
Oblivious to my pain and my suffering

Only the breeze
or the trees
or the leaves
or the ground
or the sun
or the clouds
or the stars
or the moon
or the soil
Really knows what happens here
And we do our best to live
And be normal, maybe boring
Until our lives are disrupted
By tragedy

tick tock said the hinterland clock

The liminal space
Now sucks the life
From my bones

Squeezes my lungs
Until breath catches
On the coat hooks

Where I hang my jacket
To warm
My icy exhale

Constricting like two walls
Pushing closer
You cannot keep living in liminality

Banging my fists indignantly
I cannot go back
And I'm not ready to move on

I was comfortable
In this space in between
Why do the walls want me to be

One way or the other
When I just want to be
Neither here nor there

But tick tock said the hinterland clock
Societal norms are fatigued by your stance
If you want to breathe deeply, I'll show you the door

winter tides

Light shines between clouds
The cold waves are grey and low
With rich flecks of gold
Though we are far from the sun
The wild winter tides still glow

thought ghosts

The ghosts keep trampling the sunflowers
They pick the petals from the roses and scatter them
They snap buds from tree branches
They pull forget-me-nots up by their roots
They stand in the way of sunbeams
They cover windowpanes to stop light
They slip notes under the door
so you can read your worst fears
They whisper insults as you're about to fall asleep
They repeat the same thought over and over
They hide your keys when you're late
They change your password on your internet banking
They delete your text messages
They make everything dirty so you always have to clean

But they're not dead
They can't be ghosts
They're alive within my mind

somehow i'm the one

Worn out syllables and tired consonants
Fall into the embers of the fire
Somehow I'm the one who broke them

Impatient vowels and desperate sentences
Knock on the door again and again
Somehow I'm the one who ignored them

Lonely letters and wasted words
Slink around the cloudy sky
Somehow I'm the one who sent them

Nicely spaced paragraphs and full pages
Tumble onto paper via ink
Somehow I'm the one who fixed them

empty space

This house was once full
Full of life and full of love
Now the heart is gone
Everything is packed away
All that's left is empty space

dark old day

It's a dark old day
She'd mutter with an air of vulnerable sadness
in her aged voice
When the sky was heavy with grey
Ready to send down snowflakes like feathers
or tip down rain to top up puddles
Either way, the sky was ashen black
and the world was old and filled with echoes
And you never think you're going to look out the window
with the same solemn look on your face
Hands on hips with a tut making its way out of your lips,
face lined for the paragraphs of your life story
Ready to repeat the words you've heard
The phrases that have accidentally been passed down
through the generations

And every time your voice utters them,
it connects each relative across time and space
Aligning everyone perfectly,
with a glint of nostalgia and sadness
over time gone and time yet to come
Through farming land, valleys and mountains, cities, and small seaside towns
Because no matter what time is on the clock,
or where is circled on the map
It's still a dark old day, and the need for connection never goes away

are you a tree?

The voice lingers through the woodland
Repeating each syllable with every falling leaf
These sentences were written here first
Carved through each sapling long ago
Drip-fed to the roots
You can't escape the pages that these trees hold
You can stamp all the letters into the ground
Tear each leaf to shreds
Watch the bare branches snap
Under the weight of the words
But the stories will never go

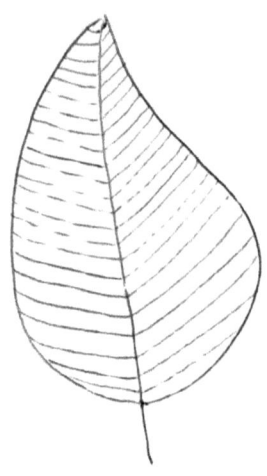

anxiety

They all keep telling me to trust
Trust yourself
Trust God
Trust the science
Where are they getting all this trust from?
Were they born with it?
Have they always just had it deep down inside?
This big ball of trust
Did they develop it day by day until they just felt calm
and everything was fine
Cause my trust hangs by a short thread which frays
a little more every day
I try to tie it on to other things to make it stronger
But it all just falls away
But I feel like perhaps I just don't have enough faith
in anyone or anything
So maybe if someone who has trust in abundance could send
me a little more
I wouldn't feel like the world was ending
Every single day

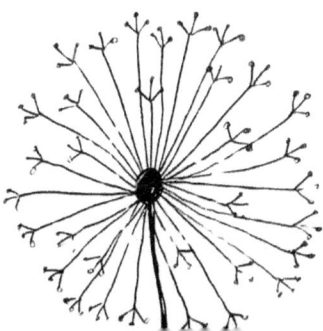

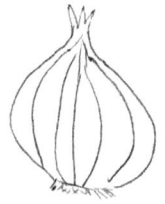

granny

I remember standing for a parade,
it might've been Remembrance Day
I remember sitting in the Blue Pearl chip shop
I remember the man who sold onions
outside the King Alf pub
I remember plastic fruit and a doll with pink hair
I remember a cupboard full of lemonade
I remember a small box of chocolate flakes
I remember a cupboard full of bits and bobs upstairs
I remember a paved garden with a wall covered in red spiders
I remember the thick brown gravy
I remember a lock on the kitchen door
I remember the tidiest front room
I remember glass sliding doors providing separation
I remember the cwtch under the stairs
I remember the china fruit
I remember scissors and Sellotape

But what I remember most is her

carrying death

The sunlight in December wanes
The air is heavy on the shoulders
Of those who carry death within them
Those hoping for good news
But knowing that it'll be wrenched from their clasped hands
Laughing at things that aren't even funny
Forgetting and remembering and panicking in a cycle
The Christmas light glow almost mocks
There's life and magic abundant
There's warm mince pies and mulled wine

But not for those who carry death within them

christmas eve

Galaxies strewn across the sky
Sparkle, just like the fairy lights
Reflected in their eyes

Unrelenting magic swirls up
Wonder, with ease, with light
Encapsulating this time

Tomorrow wrapping paper will rip and
Fall, free and tumbling
Reckless in their joy

Earth's most ancient alchemy is
Drifting, seeping across the centuries
Love in its purest form

Soon there will be sleep, despite
Excitement, anticipation of footsteps on rooftops
Full of contentment and warmth

Never forgotten, heaven on earth is
Alive, in our hearts and minds
Remembered in flame

The candle light unapologetically
Shines, just like the mass of stars
Littered across the sky

took flight

As the tired sun set
Your gossamer wings took flight
When the new moon shone
You flew just out of my sight
Towards the heavenly light

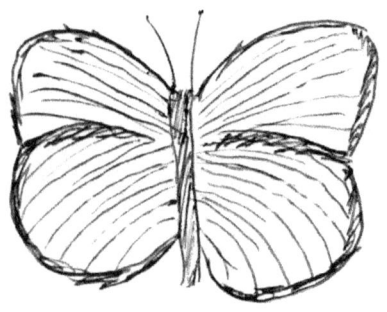

who came to get you?

Who came to get you
As I clung onto your life
Hoping death was years away

Who picked you up off my chest
And cradled you close
Telling you everything was okay

Who took you away
When the veil was so thin
Slipping away with your final heartbeat

Will you come to get me
When it is my time to go
Will you hold me close

Will you tell me everything is okay
And show me the other side of the veil
Will I know that only love exists

Will you rest your head against my chest
Until my heart stops beating
And take me with you

spirits of winter

Will you walk with me under the winter lights
Along gravel paths and tree-lined lanes
Decorate the empty branches with the grief in our hearts
Scratch names into stone with a holly leaf
Or with our fingers through frost
We can tell stories and whisper old hymns
While the cold air makes our breath ghostly and white
We can stamp our feet on a frozen stream
Breaking the seal on the other world
We can bundle up the spirits and carry them home
Singing our saddest and sweetest lullabies

from heaven to earth

I feel you with me
In the wind that moves the branches of the trees
In each leaf that falls slowly to the ground

I hear your quiet echoes
In crashing waves
In written words and music notes

I see your little glimmers
In crystal snowflakes
In flickering flames

I hold you close to my heart
In dark skies or light
In every beat or breath of my life

with gratitude to

Michelle, Lu, Paul, Tabitha, Dominic,
Robyn, Osian & Blake

And all my family & friends

about the author & artist

Elizabeth Lockwood lives with her family by the sea in Wales. She has five children – four on Earth and much missed Osian in Heaven. She has three English degrees and a love of books, which led to working in publishing and writing. Elizabeth enjoys coffee (a bit too much), reading, writing, doodling, documentaries, scenic walks, baking (and eating) cakes, and anything magical.

IG: @stars.and.leaves
Blog: starsandleaves.wordpress.com

for help:

2Wish
Support for those affected by sudden death
in young people in Wales
www.2wish.org.uk

Soft U.K.
Support Organisation for Trisomy 13/18
www.soft.org.uk

Sands
Stillbirth and neonatal death charity
www.sands.org.uk

Tommy's
Baby loss support and research
www.tommys.org

Mind
Mental Health Charity
mind.org.uk

also by turquoise quill press

We walked down to the sea front
To mark an anniversary
We let the rain drops wash our faces
Like God weeping over the memorial
Writing the letters of your name
In the slightly wet sand
So that even when it seems the world cannot recollect
We know the sea will never forget
Like us, it holds on, inhales the letters
And it breathes your memory
Out, with the break of a wave
Sending the sparks of your life
Everywhere

Waves of Stardust tells the story of Elizabeth Lockwood's fourth child, who died shortly after birth, and the grief that followed. Poems of love, loss, life and hope, this collection offers a glimpse at raw, early grief.

I can't write anymore about rain
Because nobody wants to see it
Nobody wants to hear the pitter patter
The drumming, the splash
Nobody wants it to ruin their day
Turning the white clouds grey
Nobody wants to see the windows obscured
by drips and drops
Nobody wants to go outside and get soaked through
And huff and puff at the inconvenience
So I can't write about rain anymore
Because I'll ruin everybody's day

Rain and Leaves is Elizabeth Lockwood's second book of poetry and illustrations. Her first book of poetry, Waves of Stardust, and her memoir, Little Something, are also available.

For every perceived failure, a zillion expanded worlds
Edges become blurry, as all becomes one
Grace is substantial, the rest will fade
Only Love. always Loved
Falling in Love with myself
We are the Heavens in drops of Gold

hope dealer is a book of poetry and illustrations by Catriona Messenger.

Gifting – an asking – a wanting
To know who we were before
Life excels in teaching
You to walk again
What if it's All a gift
To keep Love breathing
We allow the Divine in pain
Our wonderous collaboration on earth
Not offers of safety, But many offers of Alive

life dealer is the second book of poetry and illustrations by Catriona Messenger.

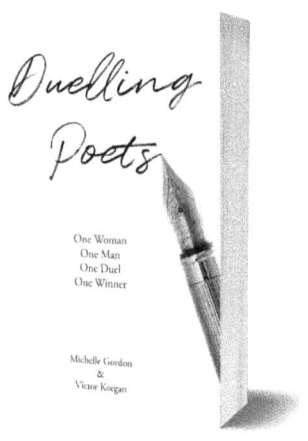

For 30 days in 2012, Michelle and Victor each wrote a poem a day, taking turns to choose the titles. Michelle is an author, who was in her late 20s at the time, and Victor, a retired journalist in his 70s. Their differing experiences and perspectives created contrasting poems, despite being written about the same theme. In Duelling Poets, we invite you to read the poems and choose your favourites, then at the end, you can see which poet wins the duel for you.

Turquoise Quill Press is an imprint of Not From This Planet

NotFromThisPlanet.co.uk

www.ingramcontent.com/pod-product-compliance
Lightning Source LLC
Chambersburg PA
CBHW040640100526
44584CB00041B/4025